DESIRE, DETERMINATION & DISCIPLINE

DR RAJENDRA MAURYA

Dedicated to

Those who wants to convert their desires into reality

Contents

Preface   *ix*

Introduction   *xiii*

1. Desire   1

2. Stages Of Desire   5

3. Importance Of Human Desires   8

4. Steps To Convert Desires Into Determination   14

5. Determination (The Will To Victory)   17

6. Why Determination   21

7. Discipline   26

8. Accomplishment Begins With Being Disciplined   29

9. Why Discipline Is Important   32

10. Examples Of Self Discipline   35

11. Self-Discipline Environment   39

12. Cost Of Being Undisciplined   44

13. Reasons For Being Undisciplined   47

14. Types Of Self Discipline   52

15. Pillars Of Self-Discipline   56

16. How To Develop Self Discipline That Last Longer   61

17. Self-Discipline Examples   84

18. Your Perfect Day   90

19. Self-Discipline And Your Health   93

20. Self-Discipline And Your Career   96

21. Self-Discipline & Your Relationships   100

22. Desire Vs Discipline Vs Determination   105

23. How 3DS Can Help To Achieve Your Goals And Dreams 107

24. Start With Simple Small Tasks And Take Actions   110

Contents

25. Final Words   113

"Discipline begins with the desire and determination to
accomplish something in your life."

Preface

Once upon a time, in a bustling city, there were three individuals named Ajay, Manoj, and Shashwat. Each of them had one thing in common: a lack of discipline in their lives. Though they possessed various talents and potential, their inability to maintain focus and structure led them down a path of failure and missed opportunities.

Ajay, a gifted musician, had dreams of becoming a renowned composer. However, his lack of discipline prevented him from practicing regularly or honing his skills. He would often procrastinate and prioritize other activities over his passion for music. As a result, he failed to meet deadlines, missed opportunities to perform, and eventually lost the interest of potential collaborators. Ajay's lack of discipline caused his talent to go unnoticed, and his dream of a successful career in music faded away.

Manoj, a promising entrepreneur, had innovative ideas and a keen business sense. However, his indiscipline life caused him to jump from one project to another without fully committing to any of them. He lacked the focus and consistency needed to see his ventures through. He would start with enthusiasm but lose interest and motivation quickly. Manoj's inability to follow through on his ideas led to a trail of unfinished projects, shattered partnerships, and missed chances for success.

Shashwat, an intelligent student, had the potential to excel academically. However, his lack of discipline in managing his time and studying effectively resulted in poor grades and missed educational opportunities. Shashwat would often procrastinate, leaving assignments and studying until the last minute. His inability to adhere to a disciplined study routine meant that he never reached his full potential, limiting his options for higher education and future career prospects.

As time went on, Ajay, Manoj, and Shashwat became disillusioned and frustrated with their lives. They saw others around them achieving their goals and fulfilling their dreams while they remained stuck in a cycle of disappointment and regret. The lack of discipline had cost them dearly, both personally and professionally.

However, one day, a realization struck them all simultaneously. They recognized that their lack of burning desire was the root cause of their failures and that need to be clearly defined if they wanted to turn their lives around. Lack of strong desire in their life further resulted in lack of determination and discipline that caused them to meet failure. Determined to break free from their self-destructive patterns, they wrote what they really want in their life and what they are passion about and committed themselves to cultivating discipline in their daily lives.

Ajay started dedicating regular time to practice their music, setting aside specific hours each day for focused practice sessions. He sought out mentors and joined musical communities to find support and accountability. Slowly but surely, Ajay regained his musical prowess and began attracting opportunities once again.

Manoj began to prioritize his projects and commit to seeing him through. He developed strategies to stay organized, manage their time effectively, and resist the temptation to jump from one idea to the next. With a great vision with discipline and determination, Manoj's entrepreneurial ventures started gaining traction, and he began to taste success.

Shashwat sought guidance from teachers and implemented a structured study routine. he broke tasks into manageable chunks, set specific study goals, and eliminated distractions. With discipline and consistent effort, Shashwat's grades improved, opening doors to new educational opportunities.

As they embraced discipline, Ajay, Manoj, and Shashwat found renewed purpose and direction in their lives. They realized that discipline was not a restriction but a tool for personal growth and success. Through their experiences, they learned that discipline was essential in achieving their goals, maintaining focus, and overcoming obstacles.

Their stories serve as a reminder that desire is starting point which lead to determination and discipline which are vital ingredients in achieving one's aspirations. Without these three things, even the most talented individuals may find themselves stuck in a cycle of unfulfilled potential. Through their failures, Ajay, Manoj, and Shashwat discovered that it's never too late to discover their desires and embrace discipline and take control of their lives, rewriting their stories with newfound determination and success.

Introduction

In life, we all harbor desires, dreams, and goals that we yearn to achieve. Whether it's obtaining a fit physique, pursuing a thriving career, nurturing meaningful relationships, or experiencing personal growth, the path to realizing our aspirations necessitates three fundamental ingredients: desire, determination, and discipline.

Desire serves as the catalyst that ignites our ambitions. It represents the profound longing and fervor within us that propels us forward. When our desire is robust, we become inspired and motivated to take action. It fuels our imagination, kindles our creativity, and maintains our focus on our objectives. Without desire, our dreams may lie dormant, and our potential may remain untapped.

Nevertheless, desire alone cannot guarantee the fulfillment of our goals. Determination is the unwavering resolve and perseverance to surmount obstacles and remain committed to our journey. It epitomizes the inner strength that sustains us during setbacks, challenges, or moments of self-doubt. Determination empowers us to persevere through adversity, learn from failures, and consistently strive for improvement. It represents an unshakeable belief in our abilities and an unwavering refusal to surrender our dreams.

Yet, even with desire and determination, success may elude us if we lack discipline. Discipline embodies self-control and consistency, which we cultivate to transform our aspirations into reality. It encompasses the ability to prioritize our actions, make deliberate choices, and adhere to a structured approach. Discipline requires us to establish healthy habits, manage our time effectively, and remain focused on the tasks at hand. It entails making sacrifices, resisting distractions, and staying committed to our long-term goals. With discipline, we can direct our efforts and energy in the right direction, maximizing our potential for success.

Desire, determination, and discipline are intertwined, each enhancing the efficacy of the others. Our desires fuel our determination, providing us with the motivation to persist. Determination, in turn, strengthens our discipline, enabling us to make the necessary sacrifices and choices in pursuit of our goals. Discipline, in reinforcing our desires, furnishes the structure and consistency necessary for progress.

Together, these three elements form a potent combination that propels us toward our aspirations. They constitute the building blocks of personal growth, accomplishment, and fulfilment. By harnessing our desires, nurturing our determination, and cultivating discipline, we can overcome obstacles, seize opportunities, and shape our lives in alignment with our deepest aspirations.

In life's journey, desire, determination, and discipline serve as guiding forces, empowering us to unlock our full potential and embrace the possibilities that lie ahead. With these three pillars, we possess the tools to pursue our dreams, conquer challenges, and forge a life that reflects our truest passions and aspirations.

CHAPTER ONE

Desire

Desire is an intrinsic part of human life. We all have desires, whether it's for improved health, a successful career, better relationships, or achieving remarkable feats. Our desires can encompass anything we yearn for.

Now, take a moment to ask yourself what you truly want from life. Not just for today or tomorrow, but also for the future - be it a year from now, five years, ten years, or beyond. To reach those levels, you need to have the desire to see yourself there.

In life, I've learned that goals can be classified into three types:

Type 1 Goals: These are goals you already know how to achieve because you have accomplished them before. For example, increasing sales volume within a specific timeframe or traveling from Place A to Place B.

Type 2 Goals: These are goals you have some understanding of and can accomplish by putting in extra effort.

Type 3 Goals: These are goals you have no idea how to achieve. You've never attempted them before, and at times, they may even feel impossible to accomplish.

Now, let me ask you something. Are you comfortable with that? Are your legs shaking in your boots? How will you achieve those goals? You may wonder what God has planned for you. Do not worry, because God is with you. Believe me, when you have a desire for something, you have already set foot on the path toward achieving your goals.

What does Lord Krishna say about goals?

"For one who has conquered the mind, the mind is the best friend. But for one who has failed to do so, the mind is the greatest enemy."

If we learn how to conquer our minds, we will be able to achieve our goals in life. And desire is the first thing that arises in our minds.

Some people merely make wishes, and their wishes never come true. They often confuse wishes with desires. However, there is a distinction between wishes and desires.

Wish vs. Desire

Wish and desire are words in the English language that are often used interchangeably, but they can carry slightly different connotations and shades of meaning.

A wish typically refers to a strong desire or longing for something that is currently beyond reach or seems unlikely to happen. It often involves a sense of yearning for something ideal or seemingly unattainable. Wishes can be related to personal goals, dreams, aspirations, as well as external circumstances or events.

On the other hand, a desire is a more general term that denotes a strong feeling of wanting or craving something. Desires can encompass a wide range of needs or wants, both tangible and intangible. They can be related to material possessions, personal achievements, emotional states, relationships, or any other aspect of life. While wishes often have a slightly more whimsical or fantastical quality, desires can be grounded in reality, reflecting immediate or tangible wants or needs.

Common Human Desires

All human activities are driven by desire. While each of us has unique differences and priorities, there is evidence that people are inclined toward several common human desires. The variations lie in how we prioritize them and how strongly we express our behaviours to fulfil those desires. Although it is clear that everyone has different goals, priorities, and values, there are some common desires shared by most human beings. Here are a few examples:

- Physical and Mental Health
- Knowledge and Information
- Financial Independence
- Family
- Transportation (e.g., cars, motorbikes)
- Lifestyle
- Sports
- Social Contact (friends)
- Basic Needs (food, water, shelter)
- Acceptance
- Prosperity
- Curiosity
- Honor
- Perfectionism
- Freedom
- Order
- Power
- Love and Romance
- Sex
- Social Status
- Peace of Mind
- Vengeance

- Security, Safety, and Stability
- Beauty
- Comfort
- Happiness
- Sleep
- Recognition and Acknowledgment
- Travel
- Sports
- Social Work
- Inclusion
- Self-Actualization (reaching one's full potential)
- Rights and Justice

These are some of the most common desires that every human wishes to have in life. There are also extraordinary desires that can lead to significant positive changes in others' lives, contributing to a better society.

CHAPTER TWO

Stages of Desire

Desire, one of the most significant words in the human dictionary, has played a vital role in our evolution and development. It has propelled us from mere survival to the highest levels of technological advancement on Earth. Desire encompasses our lives and is an integral part of society as a whole. Initially, we desire our basic human needs, and once they are fulfilled, the possibilities become limitless.

I view desire as a flame that keeps us moving towards specific objectives. It manifests in various stages, involving logical reasoning and emotional attachment.

Desires can be understood to undergo different stages or phases of development. While these stages are not universally defined or agreed upon, the following framework provides a general understanding of how desires can evolve. There are six stages of desires that everyone experiences:

Stage 1: Recognition

This stage involves becoming aware of a desire or want. It may be triggered by external stimuli, internal needs, or observing something desirable in others.

Stage 2: Intensification

Once a desire is recognized, it tends to intensify in terms of its importance and emotional impact. The individual becomes more focused on the desired outcome and experiences a stronger sense of longing or motivation.

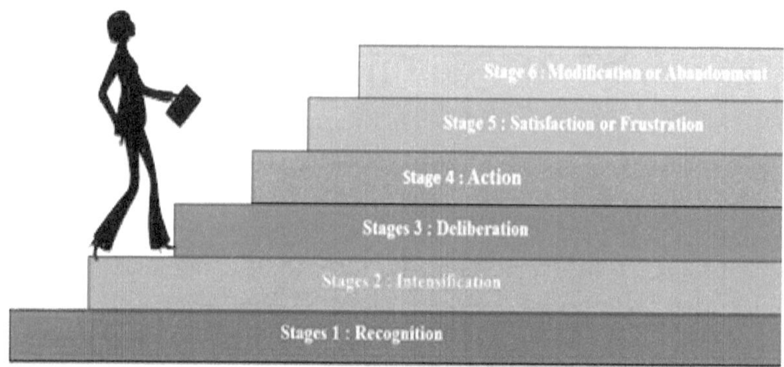

Stages of Desires

Stage 3: Deliberation

In this stage, the individual begins to evaluate the desire and considers the potential benefits, costs, and feasibility of pursuing it. They weigh the pros and cons, assess potential risks, and contemplate the effort required to fulfil the desire.

Stage 4: Action

At this stage, the individual moves beyond contemplation and takes concrete steps towards fulfilling the desire. This may involve setting goals, making plans, and actively taking measures to achieve the desired outcome.

Stage 5: Satisfaction or Frustration

Depending on the outcome, the individual may experience either satisfaction or frustration. If the desire is fulfilled, a sense of fulfilment and contentment is achieved. However, if the desire remains unfulfilled, the individual may feel disappointment, dissatisfaction, or even a renewed determination to continue pursuing the desire.

Stage 6: Modification or Abandonment

Over time, desires can evolve or change based on new experiences, shifting priorities, or personal growth. In this stage, individuals may modify their desires, adjusting their goals or redirecting their efforts. Alternatively, they may abandon certain desires altogether, recognizing that they no longer align with their values or aspirations.

It's important to note that not all desires progress through these stages linearly, and individuals may cycle between different stages depending on the nature of the desire and individual circumstances. Additionally, the intensity and duration of each stage can vary widely from person to person and from desire to desire.

CHAPTER THREE

Importance of Human Desires

Human desires play a multifaceted role in shaping our lives, motivations, and actions. They serve as powerful motivators that propel individuals to take action, set meaningful goals, and actively strive for personal growth. Desires provide the energy and determination needed to overcome obstacles and push beyond limitations. By identifying what we want to achieve or experience, desires give us a sense of direction and purpose, guiding us towards setting specific goals and working diligently to achieve them.

Fulfilling our desires can lead to deep personal satisfaction and a profound sense of fulfilment. It brings us joy and happiness, enhancing our overall well-being. When we achieve or experience what we desire, it validates our efforts and reinforces our sense of self-worth. Moreover, desires act as catalysts for personal growth and self-development. They encourage us to step outside of our comfort zones, learn new skills, and continuously evolve as individuals. By pursuing our desires, we challenge ourselves to reach new heights, discover our untapped potential, and unlock opportunities for growth that we might not have otherwise encountered.

You have a goal in your mind. You dream about it. It's a nagging thought that is constantly on your mind, but can this become a reality? All of us have dreams and ambitions; however, it takes desire to turn them into reality. Desires are the fuel for our lives.

"The shape of my life is, of course, determined by many things; my background and childhood, my mind and its education, my conscience and its pressures, my heart and its desires."- Anne Morrow Lindbergh

The power of human desires extends beyond individual benefits and has broader implications for society. Many desires are rooted in a deep yearning for progress, improvement, and innovation. They spark creativity and fuel the drive for discovery, leading to groundbreaking inventions, scientific breakthroughs, and advancements across various fields. Desires are not solely confined to personal achievements but extend to the betterment of the collective. They have been instrumental in shaping cultural and social dynamics by influencing trends, consumer behavior, and societal norms. Desires drive economic activity, shaping industries, and contributing to the evolution of social structures and values.

Furthermore, desires for love, companionship, and social connection form the basis of human relationships. They foster social bonds, promote empathy, and strengthen the fabric of communities. By pursuing these desires, we build meaningful connections with others, experience emotional fulfilment, and find a sense of belonging. Desires for love and connection enrich our lives, offering a profound source of joy, support, and shared experiences.

If a person doesn't have any desires in life, that person is no different from an animal that simply exists in this world, always searching for food, increasing its population, and eventually reaching the end of life. We are all human beings, and our intellectual capabilities and desires make us superior to other living creatures on this planet.

Burning desires hold significant importance in our lives. Here are some key points that highlight their importance:

Pursuit of True Needs: Desires help us differentiate between superficial wants and genuine needs. They guide us towards fulfilling what truly matters to us, aligning our actions with our deeper aspirations and values.

Motivation and Drive: Desires serve as powerful motivators that propel individuals to take action, set goals, and strive for personal growth. They provide the energy and determination needed to pursue aspirations and overcome obstacles.

Goal Setting and Achievement: Desires help individuals identify what they want to achieve or experience in their lives. They provide a sense of direction and purpose, guiding individuals towards setting specific goals and working towards their fulfilment.

Personal Satisfaction and Fulfilment: Fulfilling our desires can bring a sense of satisfaction, happiness, and fulfilment. Achieving or experiencing what we desire can enhance our well-being and contribute to a sense of personal satisfaction and contentment.

Growth and Self-Development: Desires often push individuals to step outside of their comfort zones, learn new skills, and seek personal growth. They encourage us to expand our horizons, discover our potential, and evolve as individuals.

Creativity and Innovation: Many desires are rooted in a desire for progress, improvement, and innovation. Human desires have been the driving force behind countless inventions, discoveries, and advancements throughout history, leading to societal progress and improvements in various domains.

Relationship and Connection: Desires for love, companionship, and social connection play a vital role in human relationships. They foster social bonds, promote empathy and understanding, and contribute to emotional well-being.

Cultural and Social Dynamics: Desires shape cultural and social dynamics by influencing trends, consumer behavior, and societal norms. They drive economic activity, shape industries, and contribute to the evolution of social structures and values.

Meaning and Purpose: Desires often reflect our values, beliefs, and aspirations, providing a sense of meaning and purpose in our lives. They help us define our identities and contribute to something larger than ourselves.

Enthusiasm and Passion: Desires ignite our enthusiasm and passion, infusing us with a sense of excitement and energy. They fuel our drive to pursue our goals with dedication and determination.

Extraordinary Life: Desires enable us to envision and aspire to an extraordinary life. They push us beyond mediocrity, encouraging us to reach for greatness and explore our full potential.

Resilience and Perseverance: Burning desires provide us with the strength and resilience to stay committed to our goals, even in the face of challenges and setbacks. They keep us motivated and encourage us to persist despite obstacles.

Unlocking Inner Potential: Desires tap into our inner resources and abilities, allowing us to harness our potential and transform it into remarkable achievements. They empower us to go beyond our perceived limits and unlock excellence within ourselves.

Bouncing Back from Setbacks: Desires act as a compelling reason to bounce back after experiencing setbacks or failures. They fuel our determination to rise above adversity, learn from our mistakes, and continue moving forward.

Reaching Our Destinations: Desires serve as guiding lights, directing our actions and choices toward reaching our desired destinations. They provide clarity and focus, helping us navigate through life with a sense of purpose and direction.

Inspiring Others: Pursuing our burning desires sets an example for others who may not have discovered their own aspirations. Our dedication and achievements can inspire and motivate those around us to find and pursue their own passions.

Creating a Better Society: Extraordinary desires have the potential to contribute to the betterment of society. By pursuing our dreams and making a positive impact, we can inspire positive change, foster progress, and create a more fulfilling and harmonious world.

It is important to note that, while desires can be powerful and influential, it is also essential to cultivate self-awareness, balance them with rationality and ethical considerations, and ensure that they align with our values and well-being.

Finding our "why" and understanding what fuels our desire to consistently chase after our dreams is a fundamental step. This driving force behind our aspirations can vary from person to person. It may be rooted in personal values, a desire for personal growth and fulfilment, a passion for making a positive impact, or a combination of various factors. Identifying our motivations helps us stay focused, resilient, and dedicated to our goals.

Dhirubhai Ambani's clear vision for the telecommunications industry and his desire to bring about a revolution in India's telecom sector fuelled his drive and determination. His son,

Mukesh Ambani, took the torch and further expanded upon that vision, resulting in the creation of Reliance Jio—a company that offers affordable services while generating substantial profits. Their "why" may have been driven by a desire to democratize access to communication, bridge the digital divide, and provide better services to the people of India.

Ultimately, finding our driving force and aligning it with our values allows us to pursue our dreams in a way that not only benefits us but also contributes positively to society. It helps us maintain a sense of purpose and fulfilment while ensuring that our desires are balanced with rationality, ethics, and the well-being of ourselves and others.

Recognizing the significance of desires, we should actively explore and identify our own burning desires. By focusing on them, we can lead a more fulfilling life and make valuable contributions to humanity. It's crucial to be aware of the reasons that lead to success and distinguish ourselves from the potential pitfalls and adverse circumstances that may hinder our journey towards achievement.

CHAPTER FOUR

Steps to Convert Desires into Determination

Napoleon Hill has been author of many best-selling books. I have read all his books. In one of his books "Think and Grow Rich" He explains how to transform desires into tangible results. Once you discover your desires you need to transmute them into determination that ultimately led you to a tangible result but converting desires into determination involves a deliberate and focused approach. Here are steps that can help in the process:

(i) Clarify Your Desires

Begin by clearly identifying and articulating your desires. Take the time to reflect on what you truly want to achieve or experience. Be specific and define your desires in clear and measurable terms. This clarity will lay the foundation for developing determination.

(ii) Set Meaningful Goals

Once your desires are clear, transform them into actionable goals. Break them down into smaller, manageable steps that you can work towards. Set realistic and achievable targets that align with your desires. Having well-defined goals provides a roadmap and direction for your determination.

(iii) Cultivate a Growth Mindset

Adopt a growth mindset, believing in your ability to learn, grow, and overcome challenges. Understand that determination requires effort, perseverance, and a willingness to embrace setbacks as opportunities for learning and growth. Embrace challenges as part of the journey towards fulfilling your desires.

(iv) Create a Plan

Develop a strategic plan to achieve your goals. Outline the specific actions, resources, and timelines needed to progress towards your desires. A well-structured plan will help you stay organized, focused, and accountable.

(v) Develop Resilience

Building determination requires resilience to overcome obstacles and setbacks. Develop resilience by maintaining a positive outlook, practicing self-care, and seeking support from others. Cultivate a mindset that sees challenges as opportunities for growth rather than roadblocks.

(vi) Take Consistent Action

Determination requires consistent effort and action. Take small, consistent steps towards your goals every day. Break down your plan into actionable tasks and commit to completing them regularly. By consistently taking action, you reinforce your determination and make progress towards fulfilling your desires.

(vii) Stay Motivated

Find ways to stay motivated throughout your journey. Remind yourself of the reasons behind your desires, visualize your success, and celebrate milestones along the way. Surround yourself with supportive and like-minded individuals who can uplift and inspire you.

(viii) Adjust and Adapt

Be open to adjusting your approach as needed. Stay flexible and willing to adapt your strategies if they are not yielding the desired results. Learn from failures and setbacks, and use them as opportunities to refine your determination and approach.

(ix) Stay Focused and Persistent

Maintain focus on your desires and goals, even when faced with distractions or temporary setbacks. Cultivate persistence by reminding yourself of the importance and significance of your desires. Keep your determination strong by staying committed to your path and not giving up easily.

(x) Review and Reassess

Regularly review your progress and reassess your desires and goals. Check if they are still aligned with your values and aspirations. Make adjustments and refine your plans as necessary to ensure that your determination remains relevant and meaningful.

Remember, determination is a mindset and a choice. By following the above steps and nurturing your determination, you can transform your desires into a driving force that propels you towards achieving what you truly want in life.

Determination (The Will to Victory)

"Winners are ordinary people with extraordinary determination."

Determination - The Will to Victory. I find no better definition of determination than this short and simple statement.

Desire is the first step towards your goals and dreams. Without desire, success becomes elusive. However, mere desire alone is not enough; you need to have a strong desire. When your desires are strong and you truly want them to become a reality, your mind propels you to the next level: determination.

I have observed countless individuals who have desires for many things, but when they realize that certain things are challenging to attain, they choose to change their path and settle for something else. Let me tell you something - by following this approach, they will never achieve anything in their life. However, if you persistently pursue your desires, goals, and dreams, and work diligently to attain them, you possess the will to victory - that is determination, a powerful weapon.

It takes a great deal of courage to keep trying again and again, no matter how long it takes or how many setbacks you face. But with determination, you will reach your destination. It's like walking in the dark with a small torch. The more you walk toward your destination, the closer you get, and as you approach, your vision becomes clearer. The determination to reach your goal makes you better. So, never lose hope and never give up until you achieve your desired goal. Dare to do things that may seem difficult for others, and do not follow the beaten path.

Case Study 1

Srikant Bolla, a young blind entrepreneur and CEO of a Rs 50-crore company from Hyderabad, exemplifies true determination in his success story. Born into a very poor family, his parents were advised to end his life because he was blind. However, destiny had other plans, and he miraculously survived. His parents provided him with the best education within their means. He faced discrimination and exclusion everywhere, even at school, where he was not allowed to play with others. Despite scoring 90% in his 10th standard exams, he was denied the opportunity to choose the science stream for 11th and 12th grade. Undeterred, he sued the state government, fought for six months, and won the case. This time, he scored 98% with a science background in his 12th board exams.

Now, Srikant desired to study engineering at the renowned IITs. However, he faced discrimination once again when he was denied an admit card to the IIT entrance examination due to his blindness. This time, Srikant made a resolute decision and said to himself, "If IIT doesn't want me, I don't want IIT either!" He applied abroad and was accepted into four of the best colleges: MIT, Stanford, Berkeley, and Carnegie Mellon. Srikant decided to pursue engineering at MIT in Boston, USA, becoming MIT's first international blind student. After completing his studies in the USA, he returned to India and launched Bollant Industries, employing over 70% physically challenged and underprivileged individuals. Today, his organization has 450 employees and is worth Rs 50 crore. His unwavering desire to become an engineer and progress in life has led him to success. In 2017, Forbes magazine named Bolla in its list of 30 under 30 across all of Asia, where only three Indians made the list. Bolla says, "I was made blind by the perception of people." When the world said, "You can't do anything," Bolla declared, "I look up at the world and say, I can do anything." Srikant's story exemplifies true determination and teaches us that with unwavering determination, there is no hurdle that can prevent us from reaching our goals.

In life, there is no difficulty that we cannot overcome if we possess true determination. Yet, many people fail on various fronts because their determination was never strong enough. Determination becomes vital because it helps us persist in the face of adversity. It allows us to walk fearlessly in our life journey with faith until we achieve our goals. As life has never been smooth for anyone, many people falter when they encounter obstacles. But with determination, we can overcome any type of obstruction.

Case Study 2

Arunima Sinha, a national-level football and volleyball player, experienced a life-altering incident that brought her close to death. Despite surviving, she had to undergo amputation of one leg, which shattered her life and presented numerous obstacles. However, even as an amputee, she discovered a desire to conquer Mount Everest. While the idea of climbing the world's highest peak with one leg may seem impossible to many, she dared to dream of reaching the summit. Through her strong desire and unwavering determination, Arunima became the **world's first female amputee to successfully climb Mount Everest.**

Determination, therefore, unleashes our creativity and imagination. To succeed in life, it is essential to set clear goals and dreams for ourselves and exert our best efforts to achieve them. Instead of rushing through life, we should proceed steadily and gradually, persisting in the face of difficulties, maintaining patience, and waiting for outcomes. Most importantly, we must have faith and courage in ourselves. Whenever discouragement sets in, we should remember never to give up and always strive to do our best.

Why Determination

A dream doesn't become reality through magic; it takes sweat, determination and hard work.

Collin Powell

Zig Ziglar once said, "I believe success is achieved by ordinary people with extraordinary determination." Indeed, having determination increases your chances of achieving a specific goal or being successful in a particular endeavor. It not only helps you remain motivated but also allows you to continue striving for the things you truly want to achieve.

Speaking from personal experience, having determination helps me stay in control and remain motivated to pursue my goals in life. Without determination, it would be challenging to push through and keep moving forward when times get tough. Therefore, it's crucial for each of us to understand what keeps us determined and to remember that answer when faced with adversity or challenging situations. The sole reason why I have been able to continue pursuing my goals over the years, despite numerous challenges that have come my way, is because I remember what makes me determined to keep moving forward.

If you possess determination and willpower for a defined objective in life, nothing can stop you from attaining that goal. While some individuals may naturally possess this trait, others may need to acquire it through practice. Once developed, however, nothing can prevent you from prospering in life. It's important to remember that the type of accomplishment you achieve depends on the goals you have defined for yourself and your level of determination. Additionally, it's crucial to understand that the journey of life is never smooth for anyone. Setbacks and breakdowns are part of the process, and we should learn from them rather than dwell on the circumstances. However, with a determined mindset, you will experience a great transformation within yourself and in your life.

Determination means making a strong resolution towards a purpose or objective. It defines the power of our will and helps us stay focused and steadfast in all our efforts. It means having the ability to stay on course, remain focused on our aims, face problems and overcome hurdles with conviction, stay aligned and firm in our decisions, solutions, and intentions, and apply the power of will to our goals, dreams, grit, strength, confidence, and courage.

Our quest for contentment and achievement begins with the right intentions and concludes when we reach our well-defined goals. What sustains our efforts along the way is our determination. Determination is what propels us toward our goals. For instance, the human landing on the moon was made possible because of determination. As I write these lines in 2023, there are individuals who have already set their determination to conquer Mars and make it a reality with firm conviction. If you are reading this book in the future, there is a great chance that humans have already landed on the red planet.

Determination is not limited to humans alone; it can also be observed in animals. They exhibit a great deal of determination to protect themselves from threats and survive against all odds. There is no doubt that determination is ingrained in advanced life forms to keep them oriented towards life and to survive in difficult situations. While determination may be referred to by other names such as tenacity, willpower, resolve, resilience, or simply determination itself, what truly makes the difference between success and failure is the power of your will and the strength of your determination. While some individuals may achieve success by luck, the majority attain it through determination. Some people give up easily, while others fight until they reach their destination.

In human beings, determination seems to be deeply rooted as part of their survival instinct and self-expression. However, not everyone possesses an equal level of determination, mainly due to various reasons. People vary in their determination to pursue their desired objectives. Some individuals easily give up, while others persist until the end. There are also those who do not even attempt to try. These variances are primarily influenced by differences in thinking, attitude, beliefs, fear, self-esteem, social and cultural influences, the strength of their desires, and the rewards or pay-offs involved. This implies that while determination may be a natural drive for survival, it can also be learned and nurtured through conscious effort, such as changing our thinking and approach.

It's important to remember that your determination greatly depends on the strength of your desires, how deeply you need something, the clarity of your goals, your sense of purpose, and your mental attitude. It also relies on your endurance for pain and suffering and your ability to manage uncertainty and ambiguity. Well-determined individuals strengthen their resolve when things don't go in their favor. They remain flexible in their plans but stay focused on their goals until they accomplish them. If there is one quality that we should all choose to accomplish our goals in life, it's determination.

Determination is the driving force that propels you forward to achieve your objectives and fulfil your dreams, even in the face of a challenging journey. It is an optimistic emotional feeling that helps you persist instead of giving up, promising to stay committed to your goals, even when it feels like a roller coaster ride.

To understand why we need determination, consider the following points:

- Determination helps you persist until you reach your goal.
- It provides the inspiration to keep moving forward.
- Determination helps you overcome setbacks and obstacles.
- It instils confidence in your abilities.
- It motivates you to work harder and maintain consistency.
- Determination enables you to bounce back from failures.
- With determination, your creativity flourishes, allowing you to find a way even in the darkest times.
- It improves your focus and productivity, helping you better prioritize your goals.
- When you are determined to achieve your dreams, it gives you the confidence to take risks.

With strong determination, we can conquer the mountains of fear, navigate through challenging circumstances, and dispel any doubts within ourselves. Determination does not mean being insensitive to reality; rather, it signifies flexibility and adaptability. A determined person remains open-minded about possibilities and opportunities while staying committed to overcoming obstacles and reaching their goals.

The power of focus is one of the most important outcomes of determination. Persistence, the spirit to continue despite adversity, is another outcome. Your determination is shaped by your faith in your goals and your abilities. Desire and determination go hand in hand, as strong desires fuel determination, making it easier to stick to a path of action and pursue it until the end. Constantly reviewing and remembering your goals and purpose can also strengthen your resolve.

Whether you call it determination, perseverance, consistency, or any other word, it is a crucial component in achieving success. The path to success is often filled with obstacles, but with determination, you continue moving forward, resolved to overcome them. Therefore, determination is vital for success, and if you aim to make a significant difference in your life, you must be determined about your goals and dreams while staying focused on them. There are countless inspiring examples of determination in the world, individuals who have paved their way to success through their unwavering resolution and grit. This is why the significance of determination cannot be underestimated, as it encourages you to dream bigger and accomplish more.

CHAPTER SEVEN

Discipline

If you have a desire for something in your life, it may or may not be fulfilled. However, if you have a strong burning desire for something, you will be determined to achieve it. Once you are determined to pursue your goals, another significant personality trait comes into play, and that is discipline. While determination plays an important role in moving towards your desired objectives, having discipline in your life is crucial to avoid falling behind on your journey.

Discipline is one of the most important personality traits found in successful individuals. It refers to a set of rules and regulations that need to be followed while undertaking tasks and activities. It is a way of being hard-working, motivated, encouraged, confident, and honest with oneself, even when no one is watching. This character trait helps individuals complete tasks within stipulated deadlines. Discipline encompasses being honest, hard-working, motivated, and encouraged throughout life. Without a doubt, this character trait is indispensable for anyone who wants to stand out from the crowd and achieve something in life.

Mahatma Gandhi, a great Indian leader, exemplified self-discipline by strictly following a trajectory of virtues such as self-restraint, self-growth, self-purification, and self-cultivation in his life. His strong desire for a free India from British rule led him to be determined to motivate people to join him in a disciplined life. His disciplined approach set an example for the vast majority of people within the country and even in other countries, like South Africa.

The role of discipline in your life is to bring uniformity, productivity, punctuality, and focus to your tasks. All successful individuals in various fields, including saints and monks who practice meditation, understand the importance of discipline. A person who is well-disciplined is undoubtedly on the right track in life. Discipline acts as the connecting bridge between goals and accomplishments; therefore, it is a crucial key to success and staying organized in life.

Akshay Kumar, a famous Bollywood actor, has been following a disciplined routine for a long time, and the results are reflected in many aspects of his life, including his health, profession, and personal life. He wakes up around 3:30 to 4 AM, engages in physical workouts, abstains from drinking and smoking, and ensures he goes to bed on time. He has balanced his professional and personal life, leading a successful and healthy life even at the age of 56.

"Life without discipline is like a ship without a radar." Therefore, the significance of discipline in our lives cannot be overlooked. It plays a vital role in shaping our character and guiding us towards success. Discipline provides structure and order, allowing us to prioritize tasks and manage our time effectively. It instills a sense of responsibility and self-control, helping us make better choices and resist distractions. Moreover, discipline fosters consistency and perseverance, enabling us to overcome obstacles and setbacks along the way.

In addition to its practical benefits, discipline also nurtures personal growth and development. By adhering to a disciplined lifestyle, we cultivate positive habits, such as regular exercise, healthy eating, and continuous learning. These habits contribute to our physical well-being, mental clarity, and overall self-improvement. Furthermore, discipline fosters a strong work ethic, teaching us the value of hard work, dedication, and commitment. It empowers us to set and achieve ambitious goals, as we develop the skills and perseverance needed to overcome challenges and accomplish great things.

It's important to recognize that discipline is not about being rigid or restrictive. It's about finding the right balance between structure and flexibility. While discipline provides guidelines and boundaries, it also allows room for adaptability and spontaneity. It helps us prioritize our actions, eliminate distractions, and focus on what truly matters. Through discipline, we can align our actions with our values and long-term aspirations, enabling us to lead a purpose-driven and fulfilling life.

To cultivate discipline in our lives, it's crucial to develop self-awareness and understand our strengths, weaknesses, and areas for improvement. Setting clear goals and creating a plan of action can help us stay on track and motivated. Breaking down tasks into smaller, manageable steps allows us to make progress consistently. Surrounding ourselves with a supportive environment and like-minded individuals can also reinforce our commitment to discipline.

In conclusion, discipline is an essential ingredient for success and personal growth. It complements determination and fuels our journey towards achieving our goals and aspirations. By embracing discipline, we gain control over our actions, develop valuable habits, and maximize our potential. It is through discipline that we can unlock our true potential and create a life of purpose, fulfilment, and achievement.

CHAPTER EIGHT

Accomplishment Begins with Being Disciplined

"Build your self-discipline and there won't be a single thing that you can't accomplish"

My mentor, Napoleon Hill, the author of the world-famous book "Think and Grow Rich," once said, "The great master key to riches is nothing more or less than the self-discipline necessary to help you take full and complete possession of your own mind." His words ring true. Discipline empowers you to take control of your thoughts, your mind, and your actions, enabling you to stay on track until you achieve your goals.

Jim Rohn wisely stated, "Discipline is the bridge between goals and accomplishment." Take a moment to reflect on these quotes. Can you now grasp the imperative nature of discipline? I hope you've found your answer.

Now, let me pose a few questions to you:

- Do you genuinely desire to achieve worthwhile goals in your life, or is success merely a wishful thought without any action behind it?
- Do you expect to attain a perfectly fit six-pack body without putting in the effort at the gym?

- Can you run a marathon without regularly engaging in running?
- Do you yearn for financial freedom and the ability to live your dream life?
- If you're a student, do you aim to secure good grades without putting in the necessary study hours?

Regardless of your specific goal, discipline is crucial for success. Without it, everything becomes more difficult to achieve, requiring additional time and effort, or possibly leading to the abandonment of your plans. Lack of self-discipline will cause you to stray from your path, rendering your efforts futile and leaving you with nothing to show for them. However, with unwavering self-discipline, you can accomplish nearly anything.

Now, direct your attention to the image below. While many of you may recognize him, some may not.

What's important, however, is to observe the transformation he underwent. The man depicted is the famous Pakistani-Indian singer, Adnan Sami, who once weighed 230 kilograms in his early adulthood. Driven by a deep desire to shed weight, he embarked on a journey of incredible discipline. As you can see in the image on the right, he successfully achieved his goal, now weighing 80 kilograms. Losing 150 kilograms is no small feat, and it certainly cannot be accomplished by sitting idly and indulging in excessive food consumption. Adnan Sami exemplified true determination and followed a strict regimen of self-discipline to achieve his remarkable transformation.

Discipline empowers you to control yourself and become the master of your life and actions. It equips you with tremendous willpower, energy, and inner strength, enabling you to remain motivated. Additionally, discipline grants you the ability to navigate challenging situations with perseverance and persistence, allowing you to continue your desired actions despite the numerous difficulties and obstacles you may encounter. Ultimately, discipline enables you to magnificently carry out what you set out to do.

CHAPTER NINE

Why discipline is Important

"We are what we repeatedly do. Excellence then is not an act, but a habit." – Aristotle

Discipline is a term that is widely known, yet only a few truly appreciate its significance. It seems to be one of those things that people either love or hate. Some view it as a good habit and an important life skill, while others see it as a burden. However, regardless of which side of the boundary you stand on, it cannot be denied that discipline plays a crucial role in one's life. Whether in personal life or in the workplace, it is a key factor in achieving success and contentment.

Discussions about the importance of discipline have taken place in fields such as psychology, philosophy, and self-help for many years. In various religions, including Hinduism, Christianity, Buddhism, and Islam, the significance of self-discipline has been emphasized. Whether in a religious, spiritual, or secular context, discipline always emerges as a topic when people seek enlightenment in their lives. It can be defined as the training of new habits and the regulation of emotions, actions, and intentional focus. Here are some points to help you understand why discipline is so important for every human being on this planet:

- Discipline builds good habits.
- Discipline helps you stay healthy.
- Discipline prevents procrastination.
- Discipline boosts self-esteem.
- Discipline makes you trustworthy.
- Following a strict discipline improves decision-making.
- Discipline helps you achieve goals and find happiness.
- Discipline helps you manage your time effectively.
- Discipline makes you a better leader.
- Discipline enables multitasking.
- Discipline helps you master your emotions.
- Discipline reduces stress and promotes a tension-free life.
- Discipline helps you become a better performer.
- Discipline makes you more reliable.
- Discipline helps you gain self-control.
- Discipline improves your ability to manage challenging emotions.
- Discipline promotes self-awareness.
- Discipline in one area positively affects discipline in others.
- Discipline helps reduce stress.
- Discipline leads to self-confidence.
- Discipline helps you avoid distractions.
- For students, discipline enhances academic performance.
- Discipline helps you think before acting.
- Discipline instils a sense of right and wrong.
- Discipline develops self-respect and respect for others.
- With discipline, you can motivate yourself without being harsh.
- Discipline is the key to success and accomplishments.
- Discipline earns respect from others.
- Discipline promotes an active lifestyle.
- Discipline helps you stick with a task until it is accomplished.
- Discipline allows you to make the most of your time.
- Discipline teaches the value of time.
- Discipline enables the accomplishment of goals.
- Discipline helps you become the best version of yourself.

The above list is endless. Discipline benefits every aspect of your life, both individually and collectively for society. It also allows people to express their attitudes and reflect their thoughts and personality. Your body and mind are nurtured through discipline. Desire, determination, and discipline pave the path to success, without requiring magical powers, innate qualities, or advanced degrees. Discipline helps resolve personal issues and fosters a peaceful and respectful civilization. It is safe to say that without discipline, there is no better life for anyone. We are all responsible for recognizing the need and importance of discipline in our lives, and it is crucial to follow discipline to make our lives better, more meaningful, and successful.

CHAPTER TEN

Examples of Self Discipline

"With self-discipline, most anything is possible."

Theodore Roosevelt

Discipline is the skill to concentrate on a task, even if it's mundane or uninteresting, and to maintain an optimistic mindset and behavior despite any opposing desires. This ability forms the foundation for not only surviving but also thriving in the complex social and economic systems of our world. The term "discipline" also encompasses the actions taken to foster discipline in oneself and others, creating an environment of order and productivity. If you possess self-discipline, you have the ability to manage yourself effectively, staying motivated and focused without relying on external reminders or supervision. In essence, your life becomes a shining example of self-discipline, where you consistently make progress towards your goals and commitments. However, it is important to acknowledge that maintaining self-discipline requires consistent effort and practice. Yet, the rewards it brings to your life are immeasurable and far-reaching.

Understanding how individuals maintain discipline in their personal and professional lives can provide valuable insights and guidance to everyone seeking personal growth and success. Disciplined individuals are significantly more likely to achieve their objectives and experience fulfilment across various aspects of their lives. Consider the following expanded list of examples that illustrate the manifestations of discipline:

- Getting up on time every day, regardless of external circumstances or temptations to hit the snooze button.
- Engaging in a regular exercise routine, prioritizing physical well-being and long-term health benefits over momentary convenience or laziness.
- Clearly defining and regularly reviewing personal and professional goals, ensuring a clear sense of direction and purpose.
- Being consistently punctual for appointments, meetings, and commitments, respecting others' time and demonstrating reliability.
- Keeping deadlines at the forefront of one's mind, actively planning and organizing tasks to ensure timely completion.
- Cultivating a habit of reading books, expanding knowledge, and gaining new perspectives.
- Sticking to a well-thought-out routine, incorporating structured activities and intentional time blocks for maximum productivity.
- Persevering through boredom or monotony, recognizing that consistency and dedication are essential for long-term success.
- Maintaining a healthy diet, consciously making nutritious choices and avoiding the temptation of indulging in unhealthy or processed foods.
- Restraining from consuming sweets or sugary treats, exercising self-control and prioritizing long-term health benefits over momentary pleasure.
- Meeting deadlines consistently, fulfilling commitments in a timely manner, and taking responsibility for one's obligations.
- Practicing patience in all aspects of life, understanding that some things take time and rushing can lead to suboptimal outcomes.
- Striving to maintain a balanced diet, consuming nourishing foods that provide essential nutrients for optimal physical and mental well-being.

- Establishing good habits, such as regular meditation, practicing gratitude, or setting aside time for self-reflection and personal growth.
- Avoiding temptations and distractions that can derail progress towards goals, employing strategies to stay focused and committed.
- Limiting screen time and consciously reducing dependence on digital devices, creating space for real-life connections and experiences.
- Setting specific time limits for entertainment consumption, avoiding binge-watching and prioritizing other meaningful activities.
- Setting personal boundaries and clearly communicating them to others, ensuring a healthy work-life balance and protecting personal well-being.
- Following through with commitments and promises made to oneself and others, fostering trust and reliability.
- Maintaining an organized physical and digital environment, creating a sense of clarity, efficiency, and peace of mind.
- Saving money and practicing financial discipline, making conscious decisions to prioritize long-term financial security over immediate gratification.
- Managing time effectively, utilizing productivity techniques and tools to optimize efficiency and make the most of available time.
- Exercising self-control in various areas of life, whether it's managing emotions, impulses, or temptations, cultivating inner strength and resilience.
- Delaying gratification, understanding the value of patience and long-term rewards, and resisting the allure of instant gratification.
- Setting and keeping commitments to oneself and others, fostering integrity and building a reputation for reliability and trustworthiness.
- Keeping a tidy home and workplace, recognizing the benefits of an organized and clutter-free environment on mental clarity and

productivity.

- Not littering anything and disposing of garbage at right place .
- Taking care of oneself holistically, practicing self-care activities that nurture physical, mental, and emotional well-being.
- Planning ahead and setting realistic and achievable goals, breaking them down into actionable steps for consistent progress.
- Establishing a reasonable bedtime routine, prioritizing sufficient sleep for overall health, cognitive function, and emotional well-being.

In summary, individuals who lead disciplined lives are more likely to achieve their objectives, experience personal fulfilment, and contribute meaningfully to their communities. Discipline empowers individuals to overcome obstacles, persevere in the face of challenges, and consistently make progress towards their goals. It is through the cultivation and practice of self-discipline that personal growth and transformation are achieved. By harnessing the power of discipline, one can become the best version of themselves and unlock their full potential.

"I could only achieve success in my life through self-discipline, and I applied it until my wish and my will became one."

Nikola Tesla

CHAPTER ELEVEN

Self-Discipline Environment

"It is better to conquer self than to win a thousand battles." Buddha

Maintaining discipline is crucial for success in personal, social, and business activities. It requires developing a positive and consistent ethical framework and cultivating a strong sense of discipline in all aspects of life.

A self-discipline environment refers to the structures, conditions, and habits that promote and support the development and maintenance of discipline. It involves creating an atmosphere that fosters focus, motivation, and the ability to resist distractions and temptations.

Regardless of the setting, discipline is essential. At home, establishing a disciplined routine helps create order and productivity. In the workplace, cultivating a disciplined culture encourages employees to fulfill their responsibilities diligently. Even in social gatherings, maintaining a disciplined environment ensures respectful interactions. When working on projects, discipline enables individuals to stay on track and meet deadlines. Wherever you are, the presence of discipline positively impacts everyone and contributes to long-term success.

Creating and maintaining a disciplined environment can be challenging, particularly for business leaders. On one hand, it is important to encourage employees to be disciplined and dedicated to their assigned tasks. However, leaders must strike a balance to avoid being perceived as overly strict or demanding. Effective leadership involves providing guidance, support, and motivation to employees, encouraging them to embrace discipline willingly and understanding their individual needs and aspirations.

Teachers also play a crucial role in instilling good manners and a sense of discipline in students. It is important for teachers to approach discipline with care and delicacy, ensuring that students feel supported and understood. By creating a safe and respectful learning environment, teachers can help students develop discipline while fostering a love for learning and personal growth.

Ultimately, creating a self-discipline environment is the responsibility of every individual. Regardless of our roles or positions, we have the power to influence and contribute to a disciplined atmosphere in our personal and professional lives. By embracing discipline, ourselves and leading by example, we inspire and encourage others to follow suit. Promoting discipline not only leads to individual success but also creates a positive and productive community that benefits everyone involved. It is our collective responsibility to create a disciplined environment and nurture it for the benefit of all.

To cultivate self-discipline in your life, there are several key elements that can contribute to creating a conducive environment:

Create a Dedicated Workspace

Designate a specific area for work or study, separate from spaces associated with relaxation or leisure. This dedicated workspace will help signal to your mind that it's time for focused work.

Establish a Routine

Structure your daily routine by setting specific times for different activities such as work or study periods, breaks, exercise, and leisure time. Stick to this routine as much as possible to develop a habit of discipline.

Remove Distractions

Minimize potential distractions in your environment. Put away or turn off electronic devices and notifications that can disrupt your focus. Create a designated space free from distractions to maintain concentration.

Accountability and Support

Surround yourself with individuals who value discipline and can provide support and accountability. Share your goals and progress with them. Consider having an accountability partner or joining a group with similar aspirations.

Set Clear Goals

Clearly define your short-term and long-term goals and break them down into actionable steps. Establish deadlines and milestones to track your progress. Having well-defined goals enhances motivation and commitment to staying disciplined.

Prioritize and Manage Time Effectively

Practice prioritization skills to identify and focus on tasks with the highest impact. Use time management techniques such as the Pomodoro Technique (working in focused bursts with breaks in between) to maximize productivity and maintain discipline.

Create Accountability

Share your goals and progress with someone you trust, such as a friend, family member, or mentor. They can provide support, encouragement, and hold you accountable for your actions.

Cultivate a Conducive Mindset

Develop a positive and determined mindset. Cultivate self-awareness and recognize thoughts and behaviors that hinder discipline. Use techniques like positive affirmations, visualization, and meditation to promote mental clarity and resilience.

Eliminate Temptations

Identify potential temptations or triggers that can derail your discipline. Take proactive steps to remove or minimize their presence. For example, if you tend to procrastinate by spending excessive time on social media, use website blockers or limit your access during productive periods.

Self-Care and Well-being

Take care of your physical and mental well-being. Get enough sleep, eat nutritious meals, and exercise regularly. When you feel energized and balanced, it becomes easier to maintain self-discipline.

Continuous Learning and Growth

Engage in continuous learning and personal development. Seek opportunities to expand your knowledge and skills, as this enhances motivation and self-discipline. Reading books, attending workshops, or taking online courses contribute to a disciplined mindset.

Celebrate Achievements

Acknowledge and celebrate your accomplishments along the way. Reward yourself for meeting milestones or achieving goals.

This reinforces positive behaviours and motivates further discipline.

Remember, creating a self-discipline environment is a gradual process that requires practice and consistency. By intentionally setting up your environment to support self-discipline and implementing strategies to stay focused, you can create an environment that minimizes distractions, supports focus, and cultivates the discipline necessary to achieve your goals.

CHAPTER TWELVE

Cost of Being undisciplined

The cost of lacking discipline can vary depending on the context and aspects of an individual's life. Here are some potential costs of being non-disciplined:

Missed Opportunities

Lack of discipline can cause individuals to miss out on valuable personal and professional opportunities, hindering progress and limiting potential for growth. Whether it's failing to take advantage of educational opportunities, career advancements, or personal development initiatives, lack of discipline can lead to missed chances for personal and professional fulfillment.

Lack of Achievement

Without discipline, it becomes challenging to set and work towards goals effectively, resulting in a lack of progress and failure to achieve desired outcomes in various areas of life. Individuals may find themselves falling short of their ambitions, dreams, and aspirations due to a lack of discipline in consistently taking action and staying focused.

Time Waste and Procrastination

Non-discipline often leads to procrastination and poor time management, resulting in wasted time, missed deadlines, and a constant feeling of being overwhelmed. When discipline is lacking, individuals may struggle to prioritize tasks, engage in time-wasting activities, and delay important actions, leading to a sense of unproductivity and frustration.

Lack of Personal Fulfillment

Discipline plays a crucial role in pursuing passions, personal growth, and living a purposeful life. Without discipline, individuals may struggle to stay committed to their dreams and aspirations, leading to a sense of unfulfilled potential and dissatisfaction. The lack of discipline can prevent individuals from taking the necessary steps to achieve personal fulfillment and find true meaning in their lives.

Decreased Productivity

Lack of discipline hinders productivity and efficiency, making it difficult to focus on tasks, meet deadlines, and produce high-quality results. Without the structure and self-control that discipline provides, individuals may find themselves easily distracted, unable to sustain concentration, and prone to procrastination. This can result in a constant feeling of being overwhelmed and lower overall productivity.

Impaired Health and Well-being

Lack of discipline can have negative impacts on physical and mental health. It becomes challenging to maintain healthy habits such as regular exercise, balanced nutrition, sufficient sleep, and stress management. Without discipline, individuals may struggle to prioritize their well-being, leading to decreased energy, increased stress levels, and various health issues over time. This can negatively affect their overall quality of life and hinder their ability to perform at their best.

Strained Relationships

Lack of discipline can lead to neglecting commitments, failing to follow through on promises, and poor communication. When individuals lack discipline, they may struggle to manage their time effectively, leading to conflicts and strained relationships with family, friends, colleagues, and partners. The inconsistency and unreliability that come with a lack of discipline can erode trust and cause disappointment, leading to strained interpersonal connections.

Financial Consequences

Non-discipline in financial matters can result in overspending, impulsive purchases, and the accumulation of debt. Without disciplined financial planning and budgeting, individuals may struggle to make wise financial decisions, save money, and invest for the future. This lack of discipline can lead to financial stress, limited financial freedom, and a lack of long-term financial stability and security.

It's important to note that discipline is not about being perfect or rigid, but rather about cultivating self-control, consistency, and focus to achieve desired outcomes. Developing discipline requires self-awareness, goal-setting, consistent action, and the willingness to overcome challenges and distractions along the way. By embracing discipline in various areas of life, individuals can reduce the costs associated with a lack of discipline and pave the way for personal growth, success, and overall well-being. Being disciplined in life can lead to improved productivity, enhanced well-being, better relationships, and increased personal fulfillment.

CHAPTER THIRTEEN

Reasons for Being Undisciplined

There are various qualities and habits that contribute to success in life, but one of the most essential is discipline. It can be incredibly challenging to accomplish goals and stay on track without self-discipline. It's important to note that self-discipline is not innate; it is something we learn and develop throughout our lives. Our behaviour is shaped by a multitude of factors, including our upbringing, environment, friends, culture, and the information we consume. Becoming a self-disciplined person requires conscious effort and determination. Even the most disciplined individuals may experience occasional lapses in commitment to their goals. However, with enough determination and a conscious effort to develop discipline, it is possible to establish a habit of self-discipline. In order to do so, it is crucial to understand the challenges that can hinder self-discipline and work towards overcoming them.

Becoming a self-disciplined person is not an easy task. It requires conscious effort and determination. Even the most disciplined individuals may experience lapses at times when it comes to committing to their desired goals. However, it is possible for anyone to make a conscious effort to develop the habit of self-discipline. The key is to have enough determination to make ourselves disciplined. Without this determination, it is likely that we will struggle to maintain self-control and discipline in the long run. In addition to willpower, it is important to identify the reasons why it can be challenging to maintain self-discipline. Once we understand these reasons, we can focus on finding solutions to overcome the obstacles that hinder our self-discipline. In this chapter, we will discuss some common reasons why people struggle with self-discipline in their lives.

Here are the main reasons for being undisciplined:

Lack of Desire in Life

One of the primary drivers of discipline is having a strong desire to achieve something meaningful. Without clear goals or aspirations, individuals may lack the motivation and drive necessary to maintain discipline. It's important to reflect on what truly matters to you and cultivate a sense of purpose in order to fuel your discipline.

Quest for Comfort and Laziness

The human brain is wired to seek pleasure and conserve energy. As a result, many people prefer immediate gratification and staying within their comfort zones. Stepping out of familiarity, venturing into the unknown, and doing things that may bring discomfort require discipline. The allure of comfort and the resistance to stepping out of one's comfort zone can hinder discipline.

Lack of Goals or Dreams

Having well-defined goals and dreams provides a roadmap for discipline. Without clear aims or dreams, individuals may lack direction and fail to take action to improve their future. Setting specific, achievable goals and breaking them down into smaller milestones can help maintain focus and foster discipline.

Unhealthy Body and Mind

Physical and mental well-being play crucial roles in maintaining discipline. A lack of self-discipline can manifest through unhealthy habits such as insufficient sleep, consuming alcohol, consuming junk food, smoking, and neglecting regular exercise. These behaviours can weaken the body and mind, leading to feelings of laziness, fatigue, and decreased efficiency. Prioritizing self-care and adopting healthy habits can boost energy levels and enhance discipline.

Lack of Willpower and Motivation

Willpower and motivation are key drivers of discipline. Without sufficient willpower and motivation, it becomes challenging to resist temptations and push through difficult tasks. Negative emotions, such as fear, self-doubt, and pessimism, can drain motivation and erode discipline. Cultivating a positive mindset, practicing self-affirmations, and seeking inspiration from role models can help bolster willpower and motivation.

Temptations

In today's world, individuals are constantly exposed to advertisements and various temptations. The allure of instant gratification can distract from long-term goals and hinder discipline. Developing strategies to manage temptations, such as setting limits, creating accountability, and practicing self-control, can strengthen discipline.

Lack of Self-Esteem

Low self-esteem can undermine discipline. When individuals lack confidence in their abilities, they may feel unworthy of success and struggle to maintain discipline. Building self-esteem through positive self-talk, celebrating small achievements, and seeking support from loved ones can foster self-discipline.

Procrastination

Procrastination is a significant obstacle to self-discipline. It involves delaying or avoiding tasks, which can lead to decreased productivity and increased stress. Understanding the underlying reasons for procrastination, such as fear of failure or perfectionism, and adopting strategies like breaking tasks into smaller, manageable steps, setting deadlines, and creating accountability can help overcome this barrier to discipline.

Fear of Failure

The fear of failure can paralyze individuals and prevent them from taking action. It hampers initiative, perseverance, and the inner strength needed for discipline. Recognizing that failure is a natural part of growth and reframing it as a learning opportunity can help alleviate this fear and promote self-discipline.

Absence of Plans and Routine

Discipline thrives on structure and routine. Without clear plans and routines, it becomes challenging to manage time effectively and accomplish tasks. Developing a well-organized schedule, setting priorities, and breaking goals into smaller actionable steps can provide the necessary framework for discipline.

Erroneous Notions

Erroneously thinking that self-discipline is difficult to attain or requires excessive denial can undermine one's efforts. It's important to reframe discipline as a tool for personal growth, success, and fulfillment rather than a burdensome chore. Embracing discipline as a positive force that empowers you to achieve your goals can help overcome these misconceptions.

Negativity

A negative environment and negative mental programming can contribute to a lack of discipline. Constant exposure to negativity can drain motivation, create self-doubt, and hinder discipline. Surrounding yourself with positive influences, seeking support from like-minded individuals, and practicing gratitude and mindfulness can counteract negativity and foster self-discipline.

By understanding and addressing these reasons for a lack of self-discipline, individuals can take proactive steps to cultivate discipline in their lives. It requires self-reflection, goal-setting, consistency, and a willingness to overcome challenges and distractions. Developing discipline is a gradual process that requires practice, patience, and self-compassion. Remember, discipline is not about being perfect or rigid but about making consistent progress and staying committed to achieving your goals. With discipline, individuals can unlock their full potential, overcome obstacles, and lead a more fulfilling and successful life.

CHAPTER FOURTEEN

Types of Self Discipline

"A disciplined mind leads to happiness, and an undisciplined mind leads to suffering."

Though there are many types of discipline that we can categorise but I could see that it can be categorized into following types based on the areas of life in which it is practiced. Here are some common types of self-discipline:

Physical Discipline

This type of discipline relates to taking care of one's physical health and well-being. It involves practices such as regular exercise, maintaining a balanced diet, getting enough sleep, and abstaining from harmful substances. Physical discipline requires consistency and commitment to healthy habits.

Time Management Discipline

Time management discipline focuses on effectively utilizing one's time and being productive. It involves setting priorities, creating schedules, and managing tasks efficiently. This type of discipline helps individuals avoid procrastination, stay organized, and meet deadlines.

Financial Discipline

Financial discipline involves managing money wisely and making responsible financial decisions. It includes budgeting, saving, avoiding unnecessary expenses, and living within one's means. Financial discipline helps individuals achieve financial stability, avoid debt, and work towards their financial goals.

Emotional Discipline

Emotional discipline is about managing and regulating one's emotions and reactions. It involves developing self-awareness, controlling anger or impulsiveness, and cultivating emotional resilience. Emotional discipline helps individuals make rational decisions, maintain healthy relationships, and cope with stress effectively.

Social Discipline

Social discipline focuses on maintaining healthy relationships and behaving appropriately in social settings. It involves practicing good manners, active listening, empathy, and respect for others. Social discipline helps individuals build and nurture positive relationships and contribute to harmonious social interactions.

Learning Discipline

Learning discipline is about developing a thirst for knowledge and a commitment to continuous learning and personal growth. It involves seeking opportunities to acquire new skills, reading books, attending seminars, and staying intellectually curious. Learning discipline allows individuals to expand their knowledge, develop expertise, and adapt to new challenges.

Goal-setting Discipline

Goal-setting discipline involves setting clear goals, creating action plans, and staying committed to achieving them. It requires breaking down goals into actionable steps, tracking progress, and making adjustments along the way. Goal-setting discipline helps individuals stay focused, motivated, and achieve desired outcomes.

Relationship Discipline

Relationship discipline involves maintaining healthy and fulfilling relationships with others. It requires effective communication, active listening, compromise, and respect. Relationship discipline helps individuals build strong connections, resolve conflicts, and foster meaningful relationships.

Spiritual Discipline

Spiritual discipline is about nurturing one's spiritual well-being and connecting with a higher power or inner self. It involves practices such as meditation, prayer, mindfulness, and reflection. Spiritual discipline provides individuals with a sense of purpose, inner peace, and guidance.

Work Ethic Discipline

Work ethic discipline is about maintaining a strong work ethic and being diligent in one's professional endeavours. It involves qualities such as punctuality, accountability, responsibility, and striving for excellence. Work ethic discipline helps individuals achieve professional success, earn respect, and contribute value in the workplace.

These are just some examples of the types of self-discipline that individuals can cultivate in various areas of their lives. Each type requires conscious effort, consistency, and a commitment to personal growth and development.

Maintaining self-discipline consistently and every day can be a challenging task. We are constantly faced with various issues that can arise unexpectedly. While we may not have control over what happens, we do have control over how we respond to these situations. It's true that practicing self-discipline requires effort, but there are strategies and techniques that can support us in our journey towards maintaining self-discipline and achieving our goals. By cultivating the right mindset and being aware of our reactions, we can view challenges as opportunities for growth. Clarifying our goals and creating a structured plan of action helps us stay focused and motivated. Additionally, making a commitment to ourselves and seeking external accountability can further enhance our self-discipline. Remember, self-discipline is a continuous practice, and by utilizing these tools and techniques, we can navigate obstacles and stay on track towards realizing our vision.

CHAPTER FIFTEEN

Pillars of Self-Discipline

"There is no magic wand that can resolve our problems. The solution rests with our work and discipline."

Jose Eduardo dos Santos

In life, nothing truly worthwhile comes easily. Long-lasting rewards are born from diligent efforts, unwavering patience, and a steadfast commitment to discipline. Just like other valuable pursuits, accomplishing your goals requires investing significant time and effort that will ultimately yield fruitful results. An effective analogy often used by experts to illustrate the power of discipline is building your body. To achieve extraordinary results, you must know your limits, stretch beyond them, and gradually build strength and resilience over time. It's important to recognize that along this journey, there will be moments of discomfort and sacrifice. However, through consistent discipline and dedication, you can emerge on the other side with a significantly brighter tomorrow. Furthermore, by cultivating discipline, you not only strengthen your own character but also inspire those around you to pursue their own paths of self-improvement.

Though it can be challenging for some individuals to develop the discipline necessary to break a bad habit, improve their well-being, or work on a demanding project, there are remedies available. One effective approach is to cultivate positive habits gradually, allowing for incremental progress. By consistently practicing these positive habits and fostering thought patterns aligned with your desired goals, you can increase your chances of success. It is essential to visualize the end result - the most rewarding or enjoyable aspects of completing a particular task or achieving a specific goal. Keeping this vision in mind serves as a powerful motivator, especially when faced with daunting challenges or ambitious dreams. By staying focused on the ultimate outcome, you can maintain your determination and persevere through obstacles that may arise along the way. Remember, discipline and goal-oriented thinking are vital elements in your journey towards personal growth and fulfillment.

Here are five pillars of discipline that you must know: -

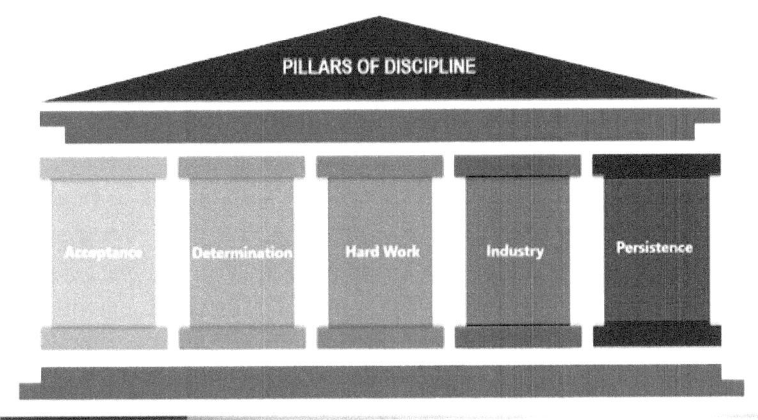

Acceptance

"When you accept your reality, you stop complaining about it and start working towards making significant changes."

The first pillar of self-discipline is acceptance. It involves sincerely acknowledging the reality of your current circumstances and accepting your true capacity for self-control. Without genuine acceptance, ignorance and denial can take hold, hindering personal growth and progress. Therefore, it is crucial to approach goal-setting with a realistic and sensible mindset. For example, when embarking on a significant project, establish reasonable deadlines that consider both your capabilities and the expectations of your clients. If you have a history of frequently extending deadlines, setting achievable targets can help rebuild your credibility, reputation, and business. The better you understand your own limitations, the more effectively you can work towards overcoming them.

Determination

"The difference between the impossible and the possible lies in a person's determination."

The second pillar of discipline is determination. It serves as the catalyst that ignites the initial boost and momentum needed to execute your plans of action. Determination is a powerful tool for self-improvement, allowing you to gradually reshape your environment to align with your goals. For instance, if your mobile phone often becomes a source of distraction while you work, practice turning it off or placing it in silent mode to maintain focus. Another source of inspiration lies in cultivating affirmative habits that naturally promote positive change. Start small, focusing on developing one habit at a time, and give yourself a reasonable amount of time, such as a month, before adding another habit to your routine. Additionally, become your own cheerleader, offering self-encouragement and refusing to succumb to self-criticism when faced with setbacks. By adopting this resilient mindset, you will persevere and continue moving forward and upward.

Hard Work

"Successful people are not gifted; they simply work hard and purposefully succeed." - G.K. Nielson

The third pillar of discipline is hard work. Unfortunately, many individuals tend to shy away from it, creating less competition and more opportunities for those who embrace diligent effort. Remember, the greater the challenge, the greater the reward. Embrace the notion that hard work involves putting in extra effort and going above and beyond in whatever task or job you undertake. By consistently pushing yourself to exceed expectations, you can stand out among your peers and achieve exceptional results.

Industry

The penultimate pillar of discipline is industry. It refers to the time and effort you invest in pursuing your mission or dreams. Effective management of your time and resources is essential to enhance your productivity and output. For example, consider comparing a drawing you completed in just 10 minutes to one that you dedicated 3 hours to. The difference in detail, refinement, and overall quality will be significant. Now, envision applying the same level of effort and time to other aspects of your life. The possibilities for growth and achievement become limitless when you allocate your energy and resources with purpose and dedication.

Persistence

"Energy and persistence conquer all things." - Benjamin Franklin

The fifth and final pillar of discipline is persistence—the unwavering ability to continue taking action despite experiencing fluctuating emotions or encountering obstacles that tempt you to quit. Persistence breeds its own inspiration. By consistently maintaining forward momentum, you will ultimately achieve tangible results that further fuel your motivation and drive. Embrace the mindset that success comes to those who persist, and let this mindset guide your actions and decisions. As a personal example, consider my commitment to running every day, even when fatigued from a hectic day or faced with unfavorable weather conditions. Establishing the habit of waking up early in the morning and heading out for a run was initially challenging. Despite numerous moments of temptation to quit, I remained steadfast. Today, running has become an integral part of my daily routine, showcasing the power of persistence in transforming habits and achieving personal growth.

Discipline serves as a powerful tool on your journey to success. By embracing acceptance, determination, hard work, industry, and persistence - the five pillars of self-discipline - you can unlock your full potential and accomplish remarkable feats. Remember, the path to success may not always be smooth or effortless, but the rewards that await are worth every ounce of effort and sacrifice. Stay disciplined, keep your vision of success in mind, and inspire others with your unwavering commitment to personal growth and achievement.

CHAPTER SIXTEEN

How to Develop Self Discipline that last longer

"Small disciplines repeated with consistency every day led to great achievements gained slowly over time."

John C. Maxwell

You know very well that you should put your phone aside and go to sleep, but more often than not, you find yourself engrossed in social media apps, watching reels, shorts, or playing games. There are also countless occasions when you get caught up in binge-watching your favourite shows on Netflix. In the morning, despite setting an alarm to wake up at a specific time, you frequently succumb to the temptation of hitting the snooze button and falling back asleep. These patterns of behaviour are not productive and will hinder your progress, leaving your desires as nothing more than unfulfilled aspirations.

It is crucial to believe and truly understand that mastering yourself is the key to achieving success in any area of life. At the core of controlling your thoughts and actions lies the development of self-discipline. It is a skill that demands consistent practice. While it is unrealistic to expect every day to be flawless, it is essential to acknowledge that each day, with its mix of failures and small victories, brings you closer to your ultimate goals.

It is worth noting that the most accomplished individuals in the world have reached their current positions because they have dedicated themselves to practicing and honing self-discipline in their lives. For many, discipline appears as a shiny objective on a distant horizon - a time when they will finally gain mastery over their messy and imperfect selves. With self-discipline, they believe they will be able to stick to their goals, such as committing to regular workouts, reducing sugar consumption, and minimizing screen time. These endeavours pave the way for the realization of their dreams. However, it is important to recognize that learning to be disciplined is not a destination or a fixed yardstick of success. Rather, it is an ongoing practice that extends throughout our lives. Practices, by their very nature, do not have an endpoint, but over time, we become increasingly skilful in them.

Numerous individuals aspire to practice discipline, but conquering this form of willpower and self-control is considerably more challenging than it may initially appear. It is crucial to be mindful of how various factors, including our upbringing, mental well-being, present circumstances, and ingrained habits, greatly influence our ability to exercise self-discipline. Consequently, learning how to become disciplined in life necessitates deliberate and conscious effort—akin to practicing self-love or facing our fears. Although the path to discipline may initially seem like an insurmountable dragon, it is always possible to make progress. Through consistent practice, you will acquire the skills and strategies required to navigate who you are as an individual and identify the areas that need further development in order to become self-disciplined. This process is essential for aligning your actions with what truly matters to you and paving the way towards the fulfilment of your dreams.

In this chapter, we will delve into various techniques and strategies that can assist you in cultivating strong discipline in your daily life. Understanding the significance of being a disciplined person is crucial, as it lays the foundation for accomplishing your goals and experiencing fulfilment.

Why Should You Care About Being Discipline Person

For some individuals, being disciplined means willingly engaging in tedious and challenging tasks that bring them joy and satisfaction. However, there are others who fail to realize that they can attain greater fulfilment and satisfaction once they achieve their desired goals. It is important to remember that discipline enables you to push yourself beyond normal limits. While there may be instant pleasures that are easier to attain, they only provide temporary satisfaction before you find yourself searching for the next thing. The truly transformative experiences that create the most meaningful positive impact in your life often come after achieving long-term goals. Disciplined individuals recognize this, even if others perceive their pursuits as boring tasks. They are willing to put in the effort because they know that remarkable outcomes await them. Embracing discipline is an essential skill that empowers everyone to overcome obstacles and conquer their fears, ultimately allowing them to attain what they desire in life.

Here are several reasons why you should care about being disciplined:

- Reduced anxiety: When you are in control of your emotions and reactions through discipline, you can focus on the tasks at hand without worrying excessively about potential mishaps or setbacks.

- Improved decision-making: Discipline helps you become a better decision-maker, leading to enhanced mental well-being.

- Goal attainment: Discipline increases your ability to accomplish both short-term and long-term objectives.

- Removal of self-disruptive behaviours: Being disciplined enables you to proactively eliminate temptations and avoid behaviours that hinder your progress. This applies to various aspects of life, such as studying, working, or managing your finances. You become better at focusing, prioritizing, and working smarter.

- Increased happiness: A disciplined lifestyle promotes progress and success, leading to increased happiness and self-confidence.

- Positive impact on relationships: Your relationships can benefit from your disciplined approach to life, as it reflects reliability, consistency, and commitment.

- Improved attitude and outlook: Research has shown that practicing discipline positively impacts your attitude and assertiveness toward tasks. This, in turn, enhances your mood and outlook on the things you need to accomplish, whether at home or in the workplace.

- Resilience: Incorporating discipline into your life fosters resilience over time, allowing you to bounce back from setbacks and challenges with greater strength.

Developing Self-Discipline for Rest of Your Life

Developing self-discipline for the rest of your life requires a new approach to effectively create positive changes. It often begins with a moment of determination when you decide to make a difference. Whether it's improving your physical fitness, nurturing better relationships, increasing productivity, or overcoming procrastination, you embark on a journey to cultivate self-discipline.

Typically, the process starts by identifying the areas you want to change and improve. You create a comprehensive to-do list, mark your calendar with important details, and perhaps even download organizational apps to assist you. In the first week, you may find yourself doing an outstanding job, staying on track, and making progress. However, as the second week approaches, you may start to relax a bit and let certain tasks slide. By the third week, you might feel like you've completely fallen off track, far from reaching your goals, and contemplating giving up.

It can be frustrating to fall short of your intentions and struggle to develop new habits. The truth is, developing self-discipline and maintaining it is not an easy process. It requires consistent effort and a different approach to ensure you stay on course and reach your desired destination.

To understand the science behind self-discipline, we need to look at the prefrontal cortex of the brain. This region is responsible for focus, emotions, and impulse control. Self-discipline is a psychological function that is connected to our impulses and emotions. It often clashes with the logical and rational part of our brains. Therefore, in order to change our behavior and become more disciplined, we need to tap into a neuroscience-backed approach that helps us rewire our brain and associate reward centres with disciplined behaviour.

Allow me to share my personal experience as an example. When I first started running and set a goal to complete a marathon, I initially felt slow and experienced soreness in my muscles and bones. However, as I continued running, I began to experience the release of endorphins and dopamine. These feel-good chemicals became associated with the physical benefits and rewards of running, which motivated me to run more.

In a similar way, by consistently practicing self-discipline, you can rewire your brain to associate positive rewards and satisfaction with disciplined behaviour. As you witness the progress, improvements, and achievements resulting from your efforts, your brain will adapt and make it easier for you to stay disciplined in the future.

Remember, developing self-discipline is a journey that requires patience, consistency, and a neuroscience-based understanding of how our brains work. By implementing these principles and consciously working towards your goals, you can cultivate self-discipline that will serve you well throughout your life.

In this chapter, we are going to show you how you can be a self-disciplined person despite where you are at present. We will discuss 30 strategies that successful people practice to stay on the right course to hit their goals and create a better life for themselves. If you use these steps, you can be sure to be a self-disciplined person and reach your desired destinations.

1. Find Out Your Strengths and Weaknesses

Is there anyone in this world who is perfect? There is no one. Each of us has weaknesses. Our weaknesses might be unhealthy food, alcohol, tobacco, an obsession with video games or social media, etc. The list goes on and on, but they all have a similar impact on us. Weaknesses don't just come in the form of a lack of self-control. Each of us has our strong suits and our weak spots. When you are self-aware, you can expand your comfort zone, but it takes constant focus along with acknowledging your flaws, whatever they may be. The flip side is that we all have many strengths as well, despite having some weaknesses. It is common for people to feel inferiority complexes, believing they are not good at anything and only focusing on their shortcomings. We need to explore our strengths and weaknesses, and instead of regretting our flaws, we should make full use of our strengths.

1. Identify Growth Regions

After determining your strength and weakness, now you need to start examining areas of your life that you would like to progress in. Maybe you have an apparent red flag, like bad results from a health screening, a bad performance assessment, or a request from your loved one to make some change.

Sometimes you may not be sure as to where to start in that case, make a note as to how you spend your time in a day now look at your schedule or mobile's screen time report for indications. Then, see what things you value the most and ask yourself whether your behaviors support those values. There are probably a few things you are doing every day that don't honor those values but remember, this is true for all of us don't worry, you won't be undertaking all these areas at once, but it's better to get the bigger picture. And once you apply self-discipline in one area of your life, your skills will get transferred to all other areas too.

3. Decide Your Goal and Start with Small

Now as you have recognized some growth areas, you should choose one to concentrate on first. You can start small by deciding on an area that you consider is easiest to accomplish. By doing this, you can feel the emotional rewards of success promptly, which will propel you to advance towards bigger goals. And if you have a bigger goal in mind, choose a smaller version of it to complete first.

For example, if you dream of doing a triathlon competition someday, you can start with individual running, swimming, and biking races first. Another example is If you want to lose 20 kg weight, start with 2 kg. you should also start by setting goals for short duration say for one week at a time.

4. Regular Physical Activity

Regular physical workouts like walking, jogging, running, cycling, exercising, doing sports, etc. provide significant benefits for health. Always keep in mind that even some physical activity is better than doing nothing. By being more active throughout your day in even simple ways, you can easily attain the recommended activity levels. The benefits of physical activity can't be ignored.

Never forget that physical inactivity is one of the leading causes of cardiac issues, noncommunicable diseases, and even mortality. Those who are inadequately active have a 25% to 35% increased risk of death comparing those people who are adequately active.

Needless to tell but I am still mentioning here some benefits of being regular in physical activity. It will :

- Help to maintain required body weight.
- Improve your cardio-respiratory and muscular fitness.
- Improve bone and functional health;
- Reduce the risk of hypertension, coronary heart disease, and stroke,
- Will help to be diabetes free and avoid various types of cancer.
- Help to keep yourself away from depression
- Reduce the risk of bone fractures if you fall down

Overall, you can be sure that if you are healthy, you not only improve your quality of life, but you are more likely to be disciplined and thus achieve your desired goals.

5. Clearly Define Your Goals & Have an Execution Plan

If you really want to have a high level of self-discipline in your life, you must have a clear vision of what you desire to achieve, just like any other goal. You also need to have an understanding of what achievement means to you. Because, if you are not sure where you are going, it's likely to lose your way or be distracted. Never forget to prioritize things. A clearly defined plan outlines each time-bound process you must go through to reach your destination. Learn to keep yourself focused. People who are successful people make use of this practice to stay on the path, emotionally connect to their mission, and ascertain a clear finish line.

6. Place Your Goals & Dreams at a Place to See Them Every Day

Writing down your dreams and goals makes them more real, and it's an important part of building discipline. So, keep it up where you can see it often and get inspired yourself. These places can be at your workplace. in your living room, in your car, in your kitchen, in your bedroom, etc. It will be better than to keep everywhere It should be everywhere you look. You should be nice to yourself and don't scare or shame yourself into your goals if they are very big; rather, be positive, joyful, and inspiring. You can also increase motivation by writing down self-discipline quotes in your diary from people who are successful and from people you admire.

7. Visualize Your End Result

You must know that that you have great chances to accomplish your goals if you write them down. And not just once rather you should write them on a regular basis. When you write down your goals it makes a connection in the real world to what's going on in your mind and serves you as a reminder. Writing can be anywhere, in a diary or as a sticky note in front of your working desk or it can be on a <u>vision board</u>. When you write down your goals and see them regularly, you will visualize them it will also give you a greater chance to succussed. Because your brain interprets images in your mind as real and creates new neural pathways to allow you to follow through. So, when you start visualizing something vividly, your brain chemistry will change as if you had actually experienced it. You should try saying affirmations loudly as "I have... or I can..." to visualize your end result and crush your feelings of insufficiency.

8. Keep a Track of Goals

Remember, if you don't define success from the beginning, then there is no way to find out whether you are making any progress or not. You should start by fixing clear goals on a daily, weekly, monthly, quarterly, and yearly basis. And from there, you must do routine recaps at the end of every day, every week, and every month to be sure that you are progressing toward your goals.

9. Be Aware of Temptations and Eliminate Temptations

There is a famous saying, "Out of sight, out of mind." Though it may seem trivial, this phrase proposes a piece of powerful advice. By just removing the biggest temptations from your surroundings, you will significantly develop your self-discipline. When I decided to be a marathon runner, many things in my life changed. If you want to have better health, you need to stop eating junk food and toss it in the trash. If you want to quit smoking? Throw out cigarettes. Same way if you want to increase your productivity at work, you need to improve the management of your To-Do's, turn off unwanted notifications and put your phone on silent mode, Prioritize things, and execute meticulously.

10. Remove Distraction

In your present work, there are so many things to distract you and make you drift from your goals. Social media is one most common thing that contributes a lot to it, especially younger generation. You need to keep yourself away from distractions around you and remain focused on your end results. Never forget that the fewer distractions, the more focused you will be on achieving your goals.

11. Develop Positive Healthy Habits

Becoming self-disciplined and inculcating a new habit can be very difficult initially, especially if you focus on the entire task in your hand. So, in order to avoid feeling intimidated, just keep it simple. Break your big goal into smaller and, doable steps, and instead of trying to alter everything at once, keep your focus on doing one thing consistently and master self-discipline with that goal in mind.

If you want to get into shape but don't exercise regularly, you can start by working out for ten or fifteen minutes every day. If you want to improve better sleep habits, you can start by going to bed five or ten minutes earlier each night and reduce it further after one week. If you want to improve your relationships start giving time to your partner. If you want healthy food, change your habits of grocery shopping and prepare meals at home. Start taking baby steps. Eventually, when your mindset and behaviour start to change, you can add more and more goals to your list.

12. Practice Daily Diligence.

No one is born with self-discipline, it's a behaviour that needs to be learned. And similar to other skills, if you want to master them, it needs practice on a daily basis along with repetition. It must become habitual for you. But there is a flip side too, the effort and focus that self-discipline requires can be tiresome and as time passes, it can be more strenuous to keep your willpower intact. The greater the temptation or resolution, the more challenging it can be to tackle other tasks that also require self-control.

So, you should begin to work on building discipline on a daily basis daily diligence in a particular area that is associated with a goal. And in order to practice daily diligence, you must have a concrete plan. Shashwat it on your calendar, or on your to-do list, keep a note on your desk, or whatever works best for you. Never forget and you need to believe that with practice, you can push the boundaries of your comfort zone every day.

13. Set Your Environment.

There are many studies conducted that show your environment makes a difference for people trying to achieve workout goals. So, before you start something, make changes to your environment in order to increase your possibilities of success. If you want to read more books, cancel your Netflix subscription, or delete social media apps from your phone and eliminate the things that might distract you. Ultimately you want to form self-discipline in any situation, removing distractions where you spend the most of your time can be helpful at first. Changing your environment is also a sign to you that something has changed as you are not just replicating your life on the same *Groundhog Day-like* loop.

14. Prioritizing Effectively

There is a tendency in every one of us to put things off sometimes, but keep putting things off for a longer time will pile up and begin to seem like an insurmountable task. When we delay things to the last minute it also causes stress and which can interfere with our ability to learn and to memorize things. We all tend to think about completing the easy tasks first, which obviously delays the slightly difficult or complex tasks and that's why prioritizing tasks is very important.

You need to decide which tasks are worthful to put the most effort into, then organize yourself to totally complete them. If you have set a study plan, you are less likely to procrastinate. Put things you really don't necessarily love at the top of your priorities, and you will be relieved and see that they are done instead of putting them off for another day.

15. Change Your Perception About Determination

If you think that you have a limited amount of determination, you probably won't surpass those limits. As I said earlier, studies show that determination can deplete over time. But can you think about changing that perception? The *Garuda Commandos* candidate in India who believes they perhaps won't make it through training, won't succeed. It's true whatever you will be your perception your mind will adapt to it, and that's why your perception to win can only take you far ahead. When you accept the mindset of unlimited willpower, you continue to grow, you will achieve more, and thus you will develop mental toughness. It's the same viewpoint as setting "stretch" goals. In brief, our internal perceptions about determination and self-control can decide how disciplined we are. If you can remove these subconscious obstacles and truly believe that you can do it, then you will give yourself an extra push of motivation toward making those goals into reality.

16. Must-Have a Backup Plan

I am sure you all have learned a lot after Covid19 pandemic. We were confined to our homes, all business activities were closed, the school was closed, shortage of food items, shortage of medicines, oxygen, toilet paper, and so on. Just think, what should have been an alarm for millions of people around the world? How many of us were ready to face this kind of situation? I think very few.

We all need to have backup plans as they are our lifeline when things don't go right as we decide. Without a backup plan, we risk digging ourselves into a costly hole. Backup plans help us to figure out what to do when things don't move as per our plan. For example, you don't get the job that you were looking for. Or your roof starts to leak and needs immediate repair. Your car started making an unusual sound and its engine need to check and get repaired.

In our life too, there are so many things that can go wrong and they will go wrong but if we have backup plans then we can be a bit relaxed as our backup plan will push through and we will become more vital than ever.

There are certain areas where we must have a back plan viz, career, finances, medical needs, personal records, etc.

17. Have Mentors or Trusted Coaches

No one is born with knowledge except Abhimanyu (Hindu Methodological character son of a great warrior like Arjun) We all learn new things after our birth and learning is a lifelong process. You should never forget that the development of expertise requires mentors, teachers, and coaches who are capable of giving constructive and sometimes painful, advice, and genuine experts are tremendously motivated students who seek out such advice. They are also experts at understanding when a coach or mentor's guidance doesn't work for them.

The top performers, that I have known so far also worked with always know what they were doing right while focusing on what they were doing wrong. They purposely picked unemotional coaches who would challenge them and drive them to a higher level of performance. The best coaches also recognize aspects of your performance that need to be improved at your next level of skill and help you in planning and preparation.

18. Learn to Forgive Yourself and Move Ahead in Life

Even with all your best efforts, intentions, and well-laid plans, you sometimes may fall short. If so, don't think it happens with you because it happens with everyone. You will experience many ups and downs, great successes and failures in your life. And the key is to keep moving. If you stumble, try to find the root cause of it by asking the five WHYs and moving on. Never let yourself get tangled in guilt, annoyance, or frustration, because these emotions will only drag you down and will impede your future progress. So, if it happens to you, you need to learn from your mistakes and forgive yourself, get your head back in the game, and move ahead in your life. Say yourself ALL THE BEST!

19. Learn and Use Pomodoro Technique

If you have not heard about the Pomodoro technique so far, let me tell you what it is.

For many of you, time may be an enemy. The nervousness activated by deadlines leads to futile work and procrastination. The Pomodoro Technique is a time management approach that was introduced by Francesco Cirillo in the late 1980s. It's a structured method that is made up of principles, tools, and values to learn how to deal with time and mold it from a malicious predator to an associate in order to boost efficiency and output. This technique is based on a series of principles built on self-awareness and observations. Developing these skills makes it possible to adjust the relationship with time and reach your goals with less effort.

As a laymen person, this method is based on 25-minute stretches of focused work then broken by five-minute breaks and there are longer breaks, taken typically 15 to 30 minutes after four consecutive work intervals.

You can also take it one step further and give the Pomodoro Technique a try and if you hold yourself responsible, you can be laser-focused and watch your productivity shoot through the roof.

20. Avoiding Decision Fatigue

Decision fatigue is mental tiredness that results from the sheer number of decisions a person has to make regularly or on a daily basis, which leads to difficulty in decision-making or poor decision-making. According to Dr. MacLean, a psychiatrist. "The more decisions you have to take, the more exhaustion you will experience and it will be more challenging for you." The theory of decision fatigue is that a human's ability to make judgments can get worse after making many decisions, as their brain will be more tired.

Mundane decisions combined with urgent and more important and critical issues cause stress and emotional exhaustion, which leads to poor choices. Decision fatigue will not stop you from making decisions but it can cause you to make bad decisions. Due to decision fatigue, you may go for impulsive shopping, you may start procrastinating or just say NO, and sometime you may get overwhelmed thus resulting in a lack of willpower.

Fortunately, there are some techniques that can help you to avoid decision fatigue and bring your life on the right track toward your goals in areas such as work, home, diet, exercise, etc.

Here are some suggestions that you can follow to avoid decision fatigue

- Learn from past decisions that you have made and analyse whether they were good or bad.
- Be conscious of your judgment and biases
- Collaborate with friends and colleagues and get their feedback on something that you need.
- Always keep in mind that time is very important so don't procrastinate of be impulsive.
- Trust your intuition and understand when to change your decision.

21. Never Undervalue Your Willpower

It may sound amazing to say that you can do whatever t your mind can think, but there is some truth to this statement. You would be surprised by what you can accomplish but you must trust yourself that if you truly believe you are capable of whatever task or obstacle is at hand. If you think that you don't have the self-discipline to successfully meet a goal, then you are likely to fall short. So, try changing your belief system of what you are capable of achieving. If you tell your mind that you have the willpower and set expectations accordingly, it will prepare you in the right direction and you are more likely to succeed. So, willpower is the key to being disciplined in your life.

22. Be Consistent and Take Small Steps

Consistency is the key to be self-disciplined, you will be on the right track as long as you are taking consistent small steps towards your end results. Let's understand it through an example. Suppose you are overweight and want to get in shape. Now, tell yourself you will go walking or jogging for at least 15-20 min every day. Now, Shashwat the dates on the calendar when you actually did it. Walking or jogging for 15 min every day will is not going to reduce your weight in fast-track mode but if you remain consistent for at least 21 days you are likely to make a habit of going out for a walk in the following days and there are chances that you may increase the time and pace that will surely help you to get rid of some extra pounds from your body. It will also help you to hold yourself accountable thus you will start practicing self-discipline on a regular basis, and make progress towards getting in shape.

23. Be Reminiscent of Why You Started

Of all the self-discipline tips mentioned in this chapter, this one can definitely help you to keep going when there are changes all around you that may check you moving towards your goals. Always keep your end goal in mind and never allow yourself to forget why you started. You need to constantly remind yourself particularly when it gets harder, and remind yourself how and why you decided to achieve this goal and what you will have achieved when you accomplish it.

Always visualize yourself as having taken overall control of your life and achieving the specific goals you have set. You may also set reminders on your phone to tell yourself how far you have come and how proud you are of yourself. Positive affirmations are also very much beneficial and helpful to stay focused on your WHY.

24. Have an Accountability Partner or Friends to Hold You

If you have a difficult time reaching your milestones, you can think that it's time to find an accountability partner. An accountability partner is a person or a friend who supports another person in order to keep the commitment or continue to progress toward a desired goal. Accountability partners has often trusted friend or someone well-known who can regularly ask an individual about their advancement or receive confessions of moral wrongdoing. You need to learn and understand how forming this kind of relationship with another person can support you reach your desired goals. You will also have someone to relate to, whether you are discussing your successes or failures.

25. Being Accountable

Accountability means an obligation or willingness to admit and accept responsibility for his/her actions. When a person takes responsibility for the outcomes of some decisions made, that person is committed to generating positive results, and some people call it "taking responsibility."

When a person is accountable, hc/she understands and accepts the consequences of their decisions and actions being taken for the areas in which they undertake responsibility. Please note that when roles and responsibilities are clear and people are held accountable, then work gets done professionally and efficiently. also, there is the possibility of constructive change and learning when accountability is followed but when roles are not clear and people are not held responsible or accountable, work is not being done properly, and in such cases, I will say there is no discipline. If you are also accountable for your decisions and actions being taken you will also be disciplined in every area of your life.

26. Failing and Trying Again

It's not that People with self-discipline never have the days where they eat sugar or junk food, spend 1 hour on social media, and lose some time all before start of the work. They definitely have these days too, but when they wake up the next morning they start over. Being Self-disciplined is the act of trying, getting failed, and trying again. You must know what is your next plan when you fail. You can also check with your accountability partner, be ready and try again the next moment.

There are numerous examples when people got failed and started again and again and got succeeded in their life. If you want to be disciplined never fail to try again after failure or any setbacks.

27. Limit Your Mindless Activities/Tasks

There are many bad habits and I will call them mindless activities or mindless tasks which are totally unproductive and you might also be involved every day. These habits really hurt our productivity, everywhere at work and in our personal life too. The more aware you are as how these activities can affect your desires and dreams, the more proactive you can be and take responsibility for your choices. It's very easy to unknowingly get involved with your phone for 20 to 30 minutes which can ruin your precious time. If you can check these urges you can stay focused and remain on top of tasks at hand and that can take you closer to your destinations. Here are some of the mindless activities: -

- Social media and other online notifications/distractions
- Checking emails frequently
- Doing another co-worker's tasks
- Checking your phone every now and then
- Doing tasks that are unrelated to you
- Opening too many tabs in the browser
- Binge-watching on Netflix/Amazon Prime or other OTT platforms
- Constantly checking work chat platforms
- Solving problems that are not yours
- Always being apprehensive that you are right
- Arranging unnecessary meetings

Above is a small list, there are many more in it. I will recommend taking a close look at your routine and tracking how often you get involved in these kinds of mindless activities.

28. Don't Wait for Things to be Perfectly Right

The things in your life that are best for you, will never come. It's not so with you rather it's the same with everyone on this planet.

It's easy to binge-watch your favorite series on TV. You came home and crashed on the couch which is effortless. The difficult thing about eating unhealthy food is putting them away and thinking about healthy eating. It is not easy to include a salad with your meal, instead, you may prefer to eat Chhole Bhature, Burgers, fries, donuts, etc. It's really hard to go get some physical exercise after a long, tiring day at the workplace.

If you keep on waiting for your schedule to clear up, if you are waiting for your kids to grow up, if you wait for good weather too for physical work out, if you want to share your knowledge waiting for free time to write a book, and so on. You will keep waiting and the right time will never come. You just need to start right now and make it happen. Disciplined people don't wait for the right time, instead, they make it right.

29. Taking Care of Yourself

Being disciplined is not worthful or may be very little if you hurt yourself to accomplish it. While following some goals may be at the cost of your overall health and may create new problems.

If you are grinding yourself for weeks or months on end to be more "disciplined," then you have missed the point.

The purpose of being disciplined is also to take full care of yourself. Taking breaks in between work, opting nutritious healthy diet, spending time in nature, and having healthy relationships will definitely rejuvenate you to help you stay focused on your goal. Don't forget that your day starts when you decide to go to bed and set your alarm in the night.

30. Make Reading a Habit

If you are really ambitious in your life and have many desires and dreams, you cannot afford to waste your valuable time. You should also not try to learn by making too many mistakes in life and to avoid this you must make use of knowledge and experience shared by other successful people. Reading books is one of the best ways to get learn many things in a short time as authors had already spent invaluable time in their life and brought their experience in the form of book for you. So, you need to make a habit of reading books every day. By reading books you not only learn new things but also you will also remain motivated for your goals.

CHAPTER SEVENTEEN

Self-Discipline Examples

After reading this chapter, you may feel motivated and have learned how to build self-discipline in your life. However, you may be wondering about some specific examples of self-discipline in everyday life. Being a disciplined person involves using your willpower to make positive choices and follow through on them.

Here are some examples of self-discipline that can help you reflect on your own habits and start working on them.

Following Healthy Habits

Discipline plays a crucial role in adopting and maintaining healthy habits. This can include going to bed early to ensure you get enough sleep, consuming nutritious foods, waking up early to exercise regularly, and avoiding harmful habits like smoking and excessive drinking. By consistently practicing discipline in these areas, you can experience significant benefits for your physical and mental well-being. Moreover, discipline also extends to practicing portion control and avoiding overeating, thereby maintaining a healthy lifestyle.

Discipline at Work

Self-discipline is essential in your professional life as it keeps you focused and aligned with your desired goals and aspirations, regardless of their size. It involves staying organized, meeting deadlines, maintaining productivity, continuously improving your skills, and seeking growth opportunities. Practicing discipline at work means being proactive and taking ownership of your responsibilities. It also means avoiding distractions, such as excessive use of social media or personal phone calls, during working hours. By maintaining discipline in the workplace, you enhance your performance, build credibility, and increase your chances of achieving career success.

Discipline in Financial Management

Earning money is not easy, and effectively managing your finances is even more challenging. Discipline plays a vital role in curbing unnecessary expenses, saving for significant life projects, and making wise investments to protect your hard-earned money. Financial discipline also entails creating and following a budget, tracking your expenses, and prioritizing your financial goals. By practicing disciplined financial management, you not only secure your financial future but also gain a sense of control over your money and reduce financial stress.

Discipline in Regulating Emotions

After a stressful day at work, have you ever found yourself lashing out at loved ones or making impulsive promises when you're feeling euphoric? These instances demonstrate the need for discipline in regulating our emotions. By developing self-discipline, we can make conscious efforts to express our emotions in a healthy manner, cope with stress, and handle unexpected disappointments with composure. This involves taking a step back, practicing self-reflection, and engaging in activities that promote emotional well-being, such as meditation or journaling. By cultivating emotional discipline, we can foster healthier relationships, improve our mental resilience, and lead more fulfilling lives.

Discipline in Relationships

As social beings, we have various relationships in our lives, such as being a parent, sibling, spouse, or friend. It's important to reflect on whether we are truly sincere and disciplined in these relationships or if we simply let them unfold without conscious effort. Nurturing healthy relationships requires discipline, as it involves actively investing time and energy, being present, communicating effectively, and practicing empathy. By practicing discipline in our relationships, we can foster happiness, trust, and a sense of belonging in our lives. This includes being accountable for our actions, honoring commitments, and consistently showing appreciation and support to our loved ones.

Discipline in Time Management

Every day, we are given 86,400 seconds to make the most of our lives. However, it is challenging to apply self-discipline and manage our time judiciously in our fast-paced society. Time is a precious resource, and learning to be disciplined in utilizing it wisely is one of the toughest tasks. By mastering the art of time discipline, we can prioritize tasks, avoid procrastination, and make significant progress toward our goals. This includes setting specific goals, breaking them down into actionable steps, creating a schedule or to-do list, and avoiding time-wasting activities. Time discipline empowers us to live life on our own terms and make the most of each day.

Self-discipline is a powerful tool that can transform your life. By practicing discipline in various areas, such as adopting healthy habits, excelling in your work, managing finances, regulating emotions, nurturing relationships, and mastering time management, you can unlock your potential and achieve the life you desire. Remember, discipline is not an overnight change; it requires consistent effort and perseverance. Embrace discipline as a guiding principle and watch how it transforms your life for the better. With discipline as your ally, you can overcome challenges, achieve personal growth, and create a fulfilling and successful life.

Incorporating self-discipline into your routine can help you become a better person and achieve your desired results. Consider adding the following practices to your life:

- Maintain a consistent sleep schedule by going to bed and waking up at the same time each day.
- Follow a regular exercise routine and stick to a fitness plan for improved physical well-being.
- Set specific goals, both personal and professional, and work diligently to achieve them.
- Adopt a healthy and balanced diet that nourishes your body and promotes overall wellness.
- Eliminate junk food and excessive sugar from your diet to support your health and well-being.
- Limit distractions, such as unnecessary use of social media and excessive TV viewing, to stay focused and increase productivity.
- Prioritize tasks and manage your time effectively to ensure important responsibilities are completed on schedule.
- Develop a habit of continuous learning, self-improvement, and reading to expand your knowledge and skills.
- Create a budget, save money, and avoid impulsive spending to achieve financial stability and meet your financial goals.
- Practice delayed gratification, understanding that long-term benefits outweigh immediate rewards.
- Take accountability for your actions and accept responsibility for any mistakes made, using them as opportunities for growth and learning.
- Combat procrastination by breaking tasks into smaller, manageable steps and taking consistent action.
- Allocate dedicated time for studying or working, adhering to a set timeline to ensure progress and completion.
- Establish a consistent routine for personal cleanliness, grooming, and dental care to maintain good hygiene.

- Practice self-control in managing your emotions, avoiding impulsive reactions during stressful situations, and seeking healthier outlets for expression.
- Save a portion of your income (at least 10%) and avoid unnecessary expenses, adhering to a well-planned budget.
- Keep your living or workspace clean and organized, minimizing clutter and developing efficient systems for orderliness.
- Set realistic goals and avoid time-wasting activities that hinder your progress or divert your focus.
- Engage in activities that foster personal growth, such as reading, listening to podcasts, watching educational videos, learning new skills, and attending personal development workshops.
- Overcome addictive behaviours and resist unhealthy temptations, cultivating healthier habits and choices.
- Demonstrate commitment, loyalty, and trustworthiness in your personal relationships, nurturing and valuing the connections you have.
- Make conscious food choices, resisting unhealthy temptations and practicing mindful eating for improved physical and mental well-being.
- Establish a consistent morning or evening routine that includes activities like expressing gratitude, practicing meditation, or journaling for personal reflection and inner peace.
- Focus on the tasks at hand, avoiding distractions, and creating a productive work or study environment to maximize efficiency.
- Value punctuality by being on time for appointments, meetings, and commitments, respecting others' time and fostering professionalism.
- Set milestones and deadlines for personal projects or hobbies, consistently working towards them to accomplish your desired outcomes.
- Practice mindfulness and stress management techniques like meditation, deep breathing, or mindfulness exercises to manage stress, cultivate inner calm, and improve overall well-being.

- Set boundaries on screen time, reducing the use of electronic devices and avoiding excessive engagement with social media or entertainment platforms.

These examples encompass various aspects of self-discipline that can be applied in different areas of your life, aligning with your personal goals and aspirations. By incorporating these practices into your routine, you can enhance your self-discipline and work towards a more fulfilling and successful life.

CHAPTER EIGHTEEN

Your Perfect Day

Everyone dreams of having a perfect life, a day that surpasses all expectations. But how many of us truly know what a perfect or ideal day means to us?

During childhood, every day felt perfect, but as we grew up, we stopped indulging in such imaginings. However, from time to time, we may wonder what our perfect day might look like. Will it revolve around having lots of money, finding peace of mind, or spending the weekend exactly as we desire? In the present moment, I would say that there is no such thing as a perfect day. However, there is something we can strive for—an ideal day that comes close to perfection.

So, I began contemplating what a perfect or ideal day might entail. The concept of a perfect day varies greatly from person to person, as it depends on individual preferences, values, and goals. Nonetheless, I can offer a generalized description of what a perfect or ideal day might look like for someone, maybe even for you.

A perfect day would start with waking up feeling refreshed and energized after a restful night's sleep. The weather would be delightful, creating a positive atmosphere. The day would be imbued with a sense of purpose and meaning, with the individual engaged in activities they enjoy and find fulfilling.

The ideal day might include spending quality time with loved ones, engaging in meaningful conversations, and strengthening personal relationships. It could involve pursuing personal hobbies or interests, such as reading, painting, playing an instrument, or participating in sports or outdoor activities.

A perfect day would also prioritize the individual's physical and mental well-being. This might involve regular exercise, yoga, practicing gratitude, mindfulness or meditation, and savoring healthy and nutritious meals. Taking breaks for relaxation, self-reflection, and spending time in nature might also be integral parts of the day.

An ideal day would strike a balance between work and leisure. It could entail making progress towards personal or professional goals, completing meaningful tasks, or engaging in creative and challenging work. Finding a sense of accomplishment and satisfaction from the day's activities would be of utmost importance.

The perfect day would ideally be punctuated by moments of joy, laughter, and gratitude. It would be characterized by positive experiences, personal growth, and a profound sense of fulfilment. Ending the day with a feeling of gratitude, reflecting on the positive aspects, and preparing for a restful night's sleep would complete the perfect day.

In addition to these aspects, a perfect day could also include acts of kindness and service to others, fostering meaningful connections with the community. It might involve learning something new, expanding knowledge and skills, or taking steps towards personal development.

Furthermore, a perfect day might encompass exploration and adventure, stepping outside of one's comfort zone and embracing new experiences. It could involve traveling to new places, trying new cuisines, or engaging in activities that bring excitement and a sense of wonder.

Embracing spontaneity and being open to unexpected opportunities could also enhance the perfect day. Allowing oneself to be fully present in each moment and appreciating the beauty and blessings that surround us can add depth and richness to the experience.

Ultimately, what constitutes a perfect day is highly subjective and will differ from person to person. It is essential to define your own values, priorities, and aspirations in order to design your perfect day accordingly. Embrace the uniqueness of your desires and create a day that aligns with your vision of perfection. By intentionally infusing your days with elements that bring you joy, fulfillment, and a sense of purpose, you can create a life that feels closer to perfect—one day at a time.

CHAPTER NINETEEN

Self-Discipline and Your Health

Self-discipline plays a vital role in maintaining good health and well-being. It is the foundation for making consistent choices and taking actions that prioritize your physical and mental wellness. By cultivating self-discipline in your health-related habits, you can experience numerous benefits and live a healthier life.

One aspect where self-discipline is crucial is in maintaining a balanced diet. It involves making mindful choices about the foods you consume, such as opting for whole, nutritious foods and limiting processed or sugary snacks. Self-discipline allows you to resist the temptations of unhealthy foods and practice portion control, which contributes to maintaining a healthy weight and reducing the risk of chronic diseases. It also involves meal planning and preparation, ensuring that you have nutritious options readily available and avoiding impulsive eating.

Regular exercise is another area that requires self-discipline. By establishing a regular exercise routine and sticking to it, you can enhance your physical fitness, improve cardiovascular health, strengthen your muscles, and boost your energy levels. Self-discipline helps you overcome common barriers such as fatigue or lack of motivation, allowing you to prioritize physical activity and reap the benefits of a consistent exercise regimen. It involves setting specific goals, whether it's completing a certain number of workouts per week, increasing the duration or intensity of your workouts, or trying new activities to keep yourself motivated and engaged.

In addition to diet and exercise, self-discipline is essential for practicing good sleep hygiene. It involves setting consistent bedtimes and wake-up times, creating a sleep-friendly environment, and avoiding disruptive activities before bedtime, such as excessive screen time. By practicing self-discipline in your sleep habits, you can ensure that you get sufficient and quality sleep, which is crucial for cognitive function, mood regulation, immune system functioning, and overall well-being. It may also involve establishing a relaxing bedtime routine, such as reading a book, taking a warm bath, or practicing relaxation techniques to signal to your body and mind that it's time to unwind and prepare for sleep.

Managing stress effectively is another aspect of health that requires self-discipline. It involves developing healthy coping mechanisms and prioritizing self-care activities that promote relaxation and stress reduction. By setting boundaries, engaging in activities like meditation, deep breathing exercises, or engaging in hobbies that bring you joy, you can effectively manage stress and enhance your mental and emotional well-being. It may also involve practicing time management and prioritization, as well as learning to delegate tasks or ask for support when needed to prevent feeling overwhelmed and stressed.

Self-discipline also plays a role in avoiding harmful habits that can undermine your health. It empowers you to make conscious choices to resist behaviours such as smoking, excessive alcohol consumption, or drug abuse. By exercising self-discipline, you prioritize your long-term health over short-term gratification, reducing the risk of various diseases and improving your overall well-being. It may involve finding healthier alternatives or distractions to replace unhealthy habits, seeking support from friends, family, or professionals, and staying committed to your health goals.

Furthermore, self-discipline helps prevent procrastination when it comes to health-related tasks. It ensures that you don't postpone important activities such as scheduling medical check-ups, seeking timely treatment, or addressing potential health concerns. By overcoming the tendency to procrastinate, you can take proactive measures to safeguard your health and well-being. It may involve setting reminders or creating a schedule to stay organized, breaking down larger tasks into smaller manageable steps, and rewarding yourself for completing health-related tasks promptly.

In conclusion, self-discipline is a fundamental aspect of maintaining good health. By practicing self-discipline in areas such as diet, exercise, sleep, stress management, avoiding harmful habits, and proactive health care, you can improve your overall well-being and enjoy a healthier and more fulfilling life. It requires commitment, consistency, and a mindset focused on long-term health and happiness. Remember, self-discipline is a skill that can be developed and strengthened over time, and the benefits you reap are well worth the effort.

CHAPTER TWENTY

Self-Discipline and Your Career

Self-discipline plays a significant role in achieving success and advancing in one's career. It involves the ability to control impulses, stay on track, remain focused on goals, and consistently work towards them, even when faced with distractions or challenges. The benefits of self-discipline in your career are manifold. Let's explore how self-discipline can positively impact various aspects of your professional life:

Goal Setting

Self-discipline helps you set clear and realistic career goals. It allows you to break down long-term objectives into smaller, manageable tasks and create a plan to achieve them. By staying disciplined and committed to your goals, you increase your chances of career advancement. Consistently working towards your goals boosts your motivation, perseverance, and overall success.

Skill Development and Learning

Self-discipline is essential for acquiring new skills and continuously improving your knowledge in your field. It involves dedicating time and effort to learning and professional development activities. By disciplining yourself to invest in your skill set, you enhance your professional capabilities and become a more valuable asset in your career. This could include attending workshops, pursuing certifications, seeking mentorship, or engaging in self-study.

Personal Branding

Discipline contributes to building a strong personal brand in your career. When you consistently exhibit discipline in your work ethic, professionalism, and results, you create a positive impression on others. Your discipline becomes a part of your professional identity, helping you stand out and gain recognition for your achievements. Consistently delivering high-quality work, meeting deadlines, and demonstrating reliability enhances your personal brand and increases your credibility in the workplace.

Consistency and Reliability

Being self-disciplined means consistently showing up and delivering your best work. It cultivates a reputation for reliability and dependability, which are highly valued in the workplace. Employers and colleagues appreciate individuals who can be counted on to meet commitments and consistently perform at a high level. By maintaining a strong work ethic, meeting expectations, and producing consistent results, you build trust and foster positive relationships in your professional network.

Productivity and Time Management

Self-discipline ensures that you maintain a consistent work ethic and consistently deliver high-quality results. It helps you establish effective routines, manage your time efficiently, and maintain a productive mindset. With self-discipline, you are more likely to meet deadlines, complete tasks efficiently, and make progress in your professional endeavours. By setting priorities, minimizing distractions, and focusing on important tasks, you optimize your productivity and achieve greater outcomes.

Resilience and Perseverance

Self-discipline helps you overcome obstacles and setbacks that may arise in your career. It provides you with the determination and resilience to keep going when faced with challenges or failures. With self-discipline, you develop the ability to learn from mistakes, adapt to changes, and bounce back stronger. It enables you to embrace a growth mindset, continually improve, and seize opportunities for personal and professional development.

Professional Image and Reputation

Self-discipline contributes to building a strong professional image and a positive reputation. It demonstrates your reliability, dependability, and commitment to excellence. Colleagues and employers value individuals who can consistently meet expectations, display self-control, and maintain a strong work ethic. By embodying these qualities, you enhance your professional reputation and open doors for advancement opportunities. A positive professional image can lead to increased visibility, recognition, and career progression.

Work-Life Balance

Self-discipline plays a crucial role in achieving a healthy work-life balance. By setting boundaries, prioritizing tasks, and practicing self-control, you can optimize your productivity while ensuring you have time for relaxation, hobbies, and personal well-being. Striking a balance between work and personal life is essential for long-term career satisfaction, preventing burnout, and fostering overall well-being. It enables you to bring your best self to both your professional and personal endeavours.

In summary, self-discipline is a valuable trait that can significantly impact your career. It enhances your productivity, professionalism, skill development, goal achievement, adaptability, personal branding, resilience, and work-life balance. By cultivating discipline in your work habits and mindset, you increase your chances of success and create a solid foundation for long-term career growth. With self-discipline, you have the power to shape your professional journey, unlock your full potential, and achieve your career aspirations.

CHAPTER TWENTY-ONE

Self-Discipline & Your Relationships

Self-discipline is not only important in personal habits and health but also plays a significant role in maintaining strong and healthy relationships. The practice of self-discipline in relationships involves creating and adhering to certain guidelines, behaviours, and principles that contribute to the overall health, happiness, and success of the partnership. Here's a deeper look at how self-discipline can positively impact your personal relationships:

Emotional Regulation

Self-discipline helps you regulate your emotions and reactions in relationships. It allows you to respond thoughtfully rather than react impulsively in heated or challenging situations. By exercising self-control, you can communicate more effectively, avoid unnecessary conflicts, and maintain a calm and understanding demeanour. This emotional balance and stability contribute to better relationship dynamics and promote healthier interactions.

Active Listening and Empathy

Self-discipline enables you to practice active listening and empathy in your relationships. It involves restraining your urge to interrupt or dominate conversations and instead focusing on understanding and validating the feelings and perspectives of your partner or loved ones. By exercising self-discipline, you show genuine interest and respect, strengthening emotional connections and fostering healthier communication.

Personal Growth and Self-Awareness

Self-discipline encourages personal growth and self-awareness, which positively impact your relationships. By practicing self-discipline, you take responsibility for your actions and behaviors, allowing you to reflect on and address any negative patterns or habits that may be detrimental to your relationship. This self-awareness promotes personal growth and allows you to become a better partner, constantly striving to improve and evolve within the relationship.

Commitment and Loyalty

Self-discipline helps you stay committed and loyal in your relationships. It involves making conscious choices to prioritize your partnership, fulfill your promises, and remain faithful. Self-discipline allows you to resist temptations that may threaten the trust and stability of your relationship. It cultivates a sense of dedication and reliability, contributing to the long-term success and happiness of your partnership. By staying committed even during difficult times, you ensure the longevity and strength of your relationship.

Continuous Growth and Self-Reflection

Discipline in relationships includes a commitment to personal growth and self-reflection. It means regularly evaluating your attitudes, behaviors, and actions within the relationship and taking steps to improve and evolve as an individual. By exercising self-discipline, you can identify areas for personal growth, address any negative patterns, and actively work on becoming a better partner. This continuous growth benefits both you and your relationship.

Respect for Boundaries

Self-discipline empowers you to establish and maintain healthy boundaries in your relationships. It involves setting clear expectations, expressing your needs and limits, and respecting the boundaries of others. By practicing self-discipline, you create a sense of safety, mutual respect, and fairness within the relationship. This fosters trust and harmony, allowing the relationship to thrive.

Time Management and Shared Responsibilities

Discipline in relationships extends to managing time and shared responsibilities effectively. It involves balancing personal and shared commitments, ensuring that both partners contribute equitably to the relationship. By practicing self-discipline, you can create routines, establish clear expectations, and maintain a healthy balance between individual needs and the needs of the partnership. This allows for a more harmonious and fulfilling relationship.

Effective Communication

Self-discipline helps you communicate effectively in your relationship. It entails being mindful and intentional in your interactions with your partner. By actively listening, expressing yourself clearly and respectfully, and avoiding communication breakdowns caused by impulsivity or emotional outbursts, you can engage in open and honest communication. This leads to better understanding, resolution of conflicts, and increased intimacy within the relationship.

Building Trust and Intimacy

Self-discipline is essential for building trust and intimacy in relationships. By consistently demonstrating trustworthiness, reliability, and accountability, you create a secure and safe environment for emotional vulnerability and connection. Self-discipline allows you to honor commitments, respect boundaries, and prioritize the well-being of your partner, which fosters a deep sense of trust and intimacy.

Conflict Resolution

Self-discipline plays a crucial role in resolving conflicts constructively within relationships. It involves approaching conflicts with a calm and composed mindset, focusing on finding mutually beneficial solutions rather than winning arguments. By exercising self-discipline, you can listen actively, express your needs and concerns respectfully, and work together to find resolutions that strengthen the relationship rather than causing further harm.

Gratitude and Appreciation

Self-discipline includes practicing gratitude and appreciation in relationships. It involves expressing gratitude for the positive qualities and actions of your partner, acknowledging their efforts, and showing appreciation for their presence in your life. By practicing self-discipline, you can cultivate a culture of gratitude and appreciation, which enhances the overall satisfaction and happiness within the relationship.

In summary, self-discipline contributes to building stronger, more harmonious relationships by fostering emotional intelligence, respect, loyalty, personal growth, effective communication, trust, intimacy, conflict resolution, and gratitude. By cultivating self-discipline in your personal relationships, you enhance your ability to communicate effectively, handle conflicts constructively, nurture deep connections, and maintain long-lasting and fulfilling partnerships. Ultimately, self-discipline helps create a healthy and thriving relationship foundation.

CHAPTER TWENTY-TWO

Desire vs Discipline vs Determination

Desire, discipline, and determination are three most important factors in your life that play distinct yet interconnected roles in achieving your goals and fulfilling your dreams and desires.

Desire

Desire refers to a strong, passionate longing or aspiration for something. It is the initial spark that ignites your goals and dreams. Desire acts as the driving force behind your motivation and provides the emotional energy that propels you forward. It is the excitement and enthusiasm that fuels your ambition and inspires you to take action.

However, while desire is a powerful catalyst, it alone is not sufficient to achieve long-term success. It must be complemented by determination and discipline.

Determination

Determination is the unwavering resolve and firmness of purpose to persevere and persistence in pursuing your goals while facing any challenges and setbacks. It is the mental and emotional strength that keeps you committed and focused to your goals, even when faced with obstacles or temporary failures. Determination enables you to maintain a positive mindset, learn from obstacles and keep moving forward with resilience.

Determination is fuelled by a deep belief in yourself and your ability to overcome any obstructions. It allows you to tap into your inner strength and push through difficulties, maintaining your focus on the end goal. With determination, you maintain the courage and persistence needed to navigate challenges and ultimately achieve your dreams and goals

Discipline

Now coming to discipline. Discipline is the practice of self-control, consistency, and adherence to certain guidelines or behaviours. It involves creating a structured approach and establishing routines to support the pursuit of your goals. Discipline helps you stay focused, resist distractions, and consistently take the necessary actions required to make progress towards what end results.

Discipline requires making conscious choices, sometimes sacrificing short-term gratification for long-term rewards. It involves setting priorities, managing time effectively, and aligning your actions with your goals. Discipline provides the necessary structure and consistency to turn your desires into tangible outcomes.

In nutshell, I will say, desire initiates your goals and dreams, providing the initial inspiration and motivation. However, determination and discipline are essential for translating that desire into action and achieving long-term success. Discipline provides the structure, consistency, and self-control necessary to stay on track, while determination keeps you resilient, focused, and committed to your goals, even in the face of adversity. All three factors work in synergy to drive your progress and turn your desires into tangible results and help you fulfil your aspirations.

CHAPTER TWENTY-THREE

How 3DS can help to achieve your Goals and Dreams

Everyone in this world wants the best things in their life, they want good health, better career, financial freedom, better relationships, good and bigger houses, social respect and recognition, respect and overall, a fulfilled life but there is a bitter truth that most people never go beyond wanting them and reason is simple they just wish to have them, instead of having a strong desire. And I will say people don't know what they desire out of their life. if you ask them, what they want in their life, their answer will be a vague reply, "I want to have lots of money, I want to have a big house, I want to have luxury car etc." If you really want to achieve best things in your life, you need to know exactly what you want. I will say you must have crystal clear picture of what you desire in your mind. Because unless you know what are your desires, you will not work for them instead you will remain in your comfort zone and you will not put your continuous effort and solid planning then a determination of true purpose furthermore a disciplined life to be awakened and developed in you.

Desire, determination, and discipline are three essential qualities that can significantly contribute to achieving your goals and dreams. Let's see how each of these attributes can help you on your journey.

As earlier explained, desire refers to a strong passion or longing for something. It is the fuel that ignites your motivation and propels you forward. When you have a deep desire to achieve a particular goal or dream, you are more likely to remain committed and take consistent action. Your desire provides the emotional connection to your goal, making it more meaningful and inspiring. And when you have strong burning desire it will push you towards determination which is the unwavering resolve and persistence to overcome obstacles and setbacks that you encounter along the way. It is the mindset that keeps you focused and committed, even when faced with challenges or temporary failures. With determination, you develop a "never give up" attitude and maintain the belief that you can overcome any obstacles that come your way. It enables you to stay motivated and find alternative paths or solutions when faced with difficulties. Once you have determination for something in your life you will not waste a single minute and follow a better routine which will lead you to be disciplined. By being disciplined you will have self-control and the ability to consistently to follow your plan and take necessary actions. Discipline will help you get involved in creating and sticking to productive habits, managing your time effectively, and maintaining consistency in your efforts. It will also help you prioritize your tasks, eliminate distractions, and stay on track toward your goals. And will enable you to make sacrifices and stay committed to long-term success rather than being swayed by short-term gratification or distractions.

Please remember, together, these three qualities form a powerful combination. When you have a burning desire, coupled with determination and discipline, you set yourself up for success. Here's how they work in synergy:

- Desire creates the initial spark, motivating you to set goals and dream big.
- Determination keeps you going, even when faced with challenges or setbacks. It helps you persevere and find new strategies to overcome obstacles.
- Discipline provides the structure and consistency required to turn your dreams into reality. It helps you stay focused, manage your time effectively, and take consistent action towards your goals.

By cultivating and harnessing these qualities, you create a strong foundation for success. However, it's important to remember that success doesn't come overnight. It requires patience, hard work, and adaptability. Along the way, you may need to adjust your approach, seek support from others, or acquire new skills. But with desire, determination, and discipline as your guiding principles, you increase your chances of achieving your goals and fulfilling your dreams.

CHAPTER TWENTY-FOUR

Start with Simple Small Tasks and Take Actions

Now that you have a burning desire to achieve your goals, it's time to take action and start moving forward. Starting with simple small tasks and taking action is a great way to develop determination and discipline in your life. Here are some steps to help you get started:

Set Clear Goals

Begin by defining your goals and breaking them down into smaller, more manageable tasks. Ensure that your goals are specific, measurable, attainable, relevant, and time-bound (SMART goals). This clarity will help you create a roadmap and identify the smaller actions required to achieve them. When setting goals, consider both short-term objectives and long-term aspirations.

Start With One Task at a Time

Choose a single task or action that aligns with your goals. Start with something small and achievable to build momentum. This could be as simple as spending 15 minutes a day on a particular activity or completing a small action related to your goal. Starting small allows you to overcome inertia and gradually build up your discipline muscles.

Create a Routine

Establish a daily or weekly routine that incorporates the task or action you have chosen. Consistency is key to developing discipline. Schedule dedicated time for your chosen task and make it a non-negotiable part of your routine. By doing it regularly, you will develop a habit that becomes easier to maintain over time. Consider finding a specific time of day that works best for you to focus on your task.

Set Reminders and Accountability

Use reminders and accountability measures to stay on track. Set alarms, use task management apps, or calendars to prompt you to complete your task. Additionally, find an accountability partner or share your goals with someone who can check in on your progress. This external support can help keep you motivated and accountable. Regularly reviewing your progress and reassessing your actions will help you stay aligned with your goals.

Celebrate Small Wins

Acknowledge and celebrate your achievements, no matter how small they may seem. Recognizing your progress boosts motivation and reinforces the habit of taking consistent action. It also helps build a positive mindset and confidence in your ability to stay determined and disciplined. Consider rewarding yourself with small treats or taking time to reflect on your accomplishments.

Gradually Increase the Challenge

Once you have established a routine and developed discipline with one task, gradually increase the difficulty or intensity of your actions. Challenge yourself to take on more complex or demanding tasks that align with your goals. This progressive approach will help you expand your capabilities and develop stronger determination and discipline over time. Pushing your limits will foster personal growth and unlock your full potential.

Practice Self-Reflection and Adjustment

Regularly reflect on your progress and evaluate what's working and what needs adjustment. Assess your level of determination and discipline, and identify any barriers or challenges that may hinder your progress. Make necessary tweaks to your routine, strategies, or goals to ensure they remain relevant and aligned with your aspirations. Continuous improvement is key to sustaining discipline and achieving long-term success.

Stay Motivated and Persistent

Maintaining self-discipline requires ongoing motivation and persistence. Find sources of inspiration that resonate with you, such as motivational quotes, success stories, or visual reminders of your goals. Cultivate a positive mindset and focus on the benefits and rewards that come from being disciplined. Surround yourself with like-minded individuals who support your journey and share similar aspirations.

Remember, building determination and discipline takes time and effort. Be patient with yourself and maintain a growth mindset. By starting with simple small tasks and gradually increasing the difficulty, you will develop the necessary habits and mindset to stay determined and disciplined in pursuing your goals and dreams, no matter how big they are. Stay focused, stay committed, and keep taking consistent action towards your desired outcome. With discipline, perseverance, and the right mindset, you can achieve remarkable results.

CHAPTER TWENTY-FIVE

Final Words

Now as you have reached to end of this book, I will say, the combination of desire, determination, and discipline is a powerful force that can propel you towards success and fulfilment in all areas of your life. By igniting your desires, nurturing unwavering determination, and practicing self-discipline, you create the conditions for extraordinary growth and achievement.

Remember that desires alone are not enough; you must back them up with the determination to persevere and overcome obstacles. Stay committed to your goals, even when faced with challenges or setbacks, and maintain a positive mindset that fuels your determination to keep moving forward.

Additionally, discipline is the key to translating your desires and determination into action. It involves creating structure, establishing productive habits, and prioritizing tasks that align with your goals. Stay focused, manage your time effectively, and remain consistent in your efforts.

As you embark on your journey, be patient with yourself and embrace the process of learning and growth. Stay open to new opportunities and be willing to adapt your strategies along the way. Surround yourself with like-minded individuals who support your aspirations and inspire you to reach higher.

Above all, believe in yourself and your ability to achieve greatness. With desire, determination, and discipline as your guiding principles, you have the power to transform your dreams into reality. Embrace the journey, embrace the challenges, and celebrate each milestone along the way. Your future is bright, and your potential is limitless. Go forth and create the life you desire.

Have a beautiful journey ahead in your life

God Bless you

I wish your dreams and desires to come true very soon.

Dr Rajendra Maurya